JUNE

NISHKA. S. TEGNOOR

INDIA • SINGAPORE • MALAYSIA

ISBN
Paperback 979-8-89588-974-9
Hardcase 979-8-89610-749-1

Contents

About the Book

The book 'JUNE' being penned by Nishka. S. Tegnoor, is a book that has expressed a little about men, how men are, how they're raised, what makes them different from women. Any part of the book doesn't mean to convey something inappropriate about women, or any individual, the writer just has posted a few thoughts about how men feel? How do they express it? Etc.

The book aims to convey that men do have feelings, men do experience pain of separation, and more. It is not that men cannot cry, they just aren't given the chance to speak their heart out. Men and women are psychologically and physiologically very different, the book only aims to convey that men too deserve a hearing ear, men can cry too, men too would need to express about how they feel.

The title is chosen for a particular reason being JUNE – MEN'S MENTAL HEALTH MONTH.

About the Author

Nishka. S. Tegnoor is a 20-year-old architecture student from Kalaburagi, Karnataka, whose passion for writing and poetry has flourished since 10. Completing her Schooling at Chandrakant Patil English Medium School and her pre-university at Sharanbasveshwar Residential PU college.

With a keen eye for creativity and writing, she has contributed to over 22 anthologies and was honored as Author of the Year by Stallions Publications for 2021-22. In this book, Nishka explores the complexities of men's mental health while also acknowledging the importance of women's emotional well-being. Her unique perspective is informed by her experiences and reflections shared on her Instagram page, @inkslingernishka. An ice cream enthusiast, Nishka often jokes that if it weren't for her love of poetry, she'd be indulging in her favorite frozen treats. With a deep commitment to exploring new ideas, she continues to inspire others through her writing.

Synopsis

As mentioned, the book aims to convey to the readers about basically men's mental health, it talks about how men's mental health is mostly ignored and how as a society are men raised.

The characters are all fictional, Aadit is a young man, who falls in love with Nalini an Entertainment Designer, their 6 years of relationship ends for a lot of misunderstandings and differences, as a man and a woman's love language is miles apart yet the two partners make adjustments and understandings to hold onto each other, however as the two understands things properly let us see how will they take it and if they will carry forward their love. Dealing with the break up, the two partners face a lot of different things, quiet portraying the same it tried to convey how men deal with it and how women do.

Reading the story let us know more about the same.

Disclaimer

The characters, the love stories, all of them are completely fictional and do not tend to target any particular community or any individual; being a very small part of the very vast topic – men and their build (psychological) the book's main aim is to convey that "Men need to be made feel that they can speak their out too, they can speak all that they feel, not necessarily men have to be cold – hearted".

Introduction

A commonly held assumption is that women are just more likely than men to have some kind of mental illness, such as depression or anxiety. However, the reality is that many men are discouraged from seeking out treatment for their mental health. Problems due to societal standards to expectations: Symptoms of mental health conditions in men may manifest themselves in more socially acceptable alternatives to sadness, such as anger. These Symptoms can include irritability, difficulty concentrating, etc. Because conversations about mental health via most of the lines ignored, and when considered, these conversations lead to center around women. I find it quite important to acknowledge and address the barriers to rare issues with men's feelings, emotions, and men's mental health.

Emotional Literacy

Emotional literacy is about being able to identify and process emotions in yourself as well as others. Women are commonly viewed as more emotional than men, where it totally depends on the individual not the gender. Women tend to be taught from an early age about to identify and communicate their emotions, while boys since childhood are asked to "man up" instead of actually asking about how are they actually feeling.

June

This book is solely aimed to focus on men's mental health; however, this does not mean or lend to ignore women, but as it is widely believed, men can't be emotional or men cannot/are not supposed to cry. All that I try to convey to my reader is "that is not men/women when it comes to mental health, and both genders need equal emotional support.

It is necessary to break the stigma of men not needing to have any emotional breakdown. Many men in society feel it is not their right to feel the emotions they are feeling and a lot of men are told to stay emotionless, saying, "'Be a man" or "Man up". The "men's mental health month" has been created by Senator Bob Dole.

Talking of men's mental health some norms include pressure on men to strong store, and independent. Their upbringing teach men to cope with these problems by themselves. Some hazards of late childhood are carryovers from earlier years, though they often take new forms.

June

"I can't deal with this anymore. I'm tired of you, us, and this relationship, which seems like having, why involvement and nowhere yours. The everyday uncared and unsolved misunderstandings, your careless behavior, your unloving. attitude, and all of it—I'm done with this. I've always you only to realize that you just don't care about anything. I bid you a goodbye for this heartless attitude of yours." Nalini yapped in a high tone and left... Aadit ignored and left, assuming Nalini will however, call him back and make things better enough. But this time Nalini had decided to never go again because what she had gone through throughout the relationship was very difficult and she was drained.

It took Nalini a lot of time to get over who she had loved beyond herself—who she made her whole world. Aadit's ego stopped him from reaching who he loved more than he knew, his strength and his weakness. His ego made him let her go and behave like he was unaffected by their separation.

Two months passed with no contact between the two. However, Nalini had already given up on their relationship, and though she was living with difficulty after separation, she had decided to not make any efforts towards Aadit anymore.

Aadit himself was finding it difficult to live without Nalini, all that was stopping him from reaching out to her was his ego, and his immense love for her kept him waiting for her to come back to him, but either way neither he got back to her nor did she contact him. However, his misbelief that she will never leave him kept consuming him by waiting on her return.

Aadit, Mr. Ranjiv Rasaih, a well known entrepreneur's son. They are well known, powerful and a cultural family, possessing huge respect based from a town Prithvidur, their businesses, and charities were spread in Nishantpuri as well as Anandavan.

Around 621 KM away from Prithvidhur was Celestial city, the city of dreams, the city that had opportunities for everyone, the city that had limitless competition in every single field of work.

Nalini, to leave behind all that happened and to begin anew, try new things and get over the past, moved to Celeistial city from Prithvidur and started living with her friend Sara in Moonlight Meadows Apartments at the Ivywood Bay street of the city.

Nalini has been a voracious reader, a book geek. She also is keen and fascinated about music and however her profession and her passions were miles apart. She had pursued bachelors in Entertainment design, diving into her interests to build a career that she had dreamt of.

After moving to Celestial city Nalini's priority was to get over the break up, move on and make her career all settled. However, going through heartbreak has made her decide to no further have any sort of love/relationship, she needed self time, care and everything that'd make her a bit happier or busier as of to make sure the break up doesn't consuming her. Aadit however continued his routine masking up that he is unaffected by the breakup, as a responsible man who had taken up responsibilities at the age of 16 – at the age of games, fun & partying, he took over his dad's business, due to an unfortunate accident that cost Mr. Rasaih's life at the age of 42. Aadit had the responsibility of his younger brother and sister and his mom; all that of his teenage life turned to a responsibility filled life, bravely did Aadit make it all upto himself, his family and the people of Prithvidur by taking up their business to higher heights at the age where most of them pre-assumed of the losses of Rasiah's business, however, tackling and facing the negativity, the bad assumptions, and the trials of people to fail Aadit, he came through it all, strongly, bravely, and wisely. He only believed what he had been put through for the past 3 years since his dad's demise made him a more capable man, bringing him out stronger and wiser.

Throughout the years he could never completely express himself to anyone, being the responsible man. The same way did the breakup keep him. However, the way found to let all of it out was through anger, generally being short tempered about even the smallest wrong going or an inconvenience, which he'd already have awareness about that it is not as bad/wrong as he is show casing his rage and aggression.

Nalini was a business man's daughter who dreamt of life to be a fairy tale and less did she know fairy tales were only dreams. After the break up, on a Friday evening, she joined a baking workshop to engage herself in what interests her; it was more likely for her to move on and get over the love of about 6 years. Not at all interested in marriage, Nalini rejected the proposals of an arranged marriage set up that her mom tried to convince her for; being told the reason she wants to explore her field of interests and timely focus on her profession.

The baking course was a 3-month workshop in which Nalini's major goals were about learning to bake Aadit's favorite cheesecake, while Sara's comrade tried convincing her that "moving on over Aadit will mean that you will have to stop thinking about him in all that you do, you need to ignore about his likes, dislikes, his favorite food, color, City, Country and everything. You can't forget if you do this. The baking workshop that you joined isn't for you to always remind yourself about his likes and it is the reason for you to get over the break up, you can never get over it if you focus on learning to bake his favorite cake in the course you joined to forget him. There are many more things you can learn, like your favorite brownie or My favorite Choco lava brownie, just anything except for a cheesecake which Aadit loves", however Nalini said "I don't understand it, but what he loves, learning that is a kind of happiness, maybe I shall learn it as a last string of our relationship, trust me I might cry for the first time I bake his favorite cheesecake but eventually it'll remain with me as a memory or 'THE LAST STRING OF THE RELATIONSHIP' one last connectivity between me & Aadit before we begin all new life or just whatever, I believe learning to bake his favorite Cheesecake will make me happier than learning anything else", Sara hugged Nalini and told her, do what you'd love, if it hurts I'm always here to hear you, hug you and help you" Nalini thanked Sara with a tighter hug and the both started cooking, planning for a Movie night, along some ice cream and some sides. The two friends cooked a very tasty mixed vegetable curry and some vegetable rice. Once they looked the food and had their dinner with some chit-chatting they did their dishes, and freshened up, like the cautious women, Nalini and Sara continued their night skincare routine with utmost urge of a having a perfect skin, the dream of every girl, at around 9:30 PM both the friends then started discussing about the movie, both of them started to choose one, and seeing the long list of movies to choose one to watch and call it a night, a movie night. They then decided after 15 minutes that they do not want to watch a biopic, thriller or horror or any documentary, they kept for options – drama, romance, rom-com & action, soon in 5 more minutes they deducted action from the choice. After 30 solid minutes Nalini and Sara came to a final decision, like it was a major decision to choose a movie to watch for the night, however, both typically chose a romance, fictional-romcom kind of a movie, "Heart strings and Hichkiyaan", the movie started on with a group of college friends living life to the fullest, making memories; the group of three travelled to Varunagiri a place that almost looked heaven, a place with Very divinely nature, the place they were actually looking for, peace and silence, away from College, home and all the unnecessary situations in and around. Advait, Reyansh and Sanay were less of friends and more like siblings, the story was a bind of friendship, hardships, fun, never giving up and love story; that showcase three kinds of love lives with the three superhero like men, where Advait falls in love in his college days, on the trip to Varunagiri, love with a beautiful girl who's been a old school lover, she was so adorable that Advait couldn't Stop himself from falling in love with Navya, starting from Varunagiri dreaming of a togetherness till the end of life, believing in love through all the hardships, ups and downs of relationship. Being through all of it, one of the three musketeers got married to the love of his life, showcasing a beautiful love between Advait and Navya.

Reyansh being a very humble yet cold kind of a man, who have been fun loving and caring, a family man, focused on being the most successful without sacrificing any love and time to family. Fixed in an arranged marriage set up, Reyansh started falling in love with Samitha an Architect, a family oriented beautiful girl passionate about music, with a very soothing voice. He was very thankful to god for bringing to life his spouse, Samitha. They being a happy loving couple, became a family of being a perfect frame of "HAPPILY EVER AFTER".

Sanay, was a very adventurous person, among the three, but had been through a breakup previously for what he's been away from love since 3 years. but love is never a one time story, if it is then it is not less than a fiction – having to find the love of line in the first go.

Sanay, Advait and Reyansh had a Junior Nabhya who's been quite close to the three. Nabhya has been a cheerful, loving woman, an enthusiastic girl aspiring to be an entrepreneur. Neither Nabhya nor Sanay ever knew they'd fall in love. Sanay had made up his mind that there shall be no love anymore, but destiny had other plans, for both the love birds.

Advait and Reyansh made it obvious to Sanay about how he loves Nabhya without himself realizing it, at the same time, Nabhya also prepared all herself to confess her love to Sanay, before he leaves college and their friendship eventually cuts off. Gathering much of courage she asked him for a coffee; deciding to write a letter because it'd be difficult to speak it up. The two catching up that evening at Nabhya's favorite coffee shop, the two expressed their sadness of not being able to see each other everyday now onwards. Nabhya gently propelled the letter to Sanay, nodding her head, conveying him to read it, before he opens her letter, he presented her a bouquet with a Small piece of paper, he then opened the letter, by time, she read "Hi Nabhya, I'm not into much of writing long paragraphs but I had to tell you that I love you I might have fallen in love with since the first time we spoke, now that I'm sure of it I confess it to you, I've no hurry or any kind of pressure, the decision is up to you."

Alike every, or almost every girl in love, that loves expressing her affection in words Nabhya did the same, through a letter. While Nabhya was reading what Sanay had written, Sanay patiently kept waiting without reading what Nabhya had written, and as Nabhya finished reading Sanay's letter, she said "all that I've to say is in the letter and maybe the answer of your letter too" and sipped her favorite coffee.

Sanay being a bit confused, hoping for love, opened the letter and it said "Hi Sanay, I'm very thankful for you for being so supportive in college, and always giving me a sense of protection in every minor to bigger things. I'm thankful to three of you for being the best to me through your college, in or out of college, academically and personally and every possible way. Compared to Advait and Reyansh you've been very close to me Sanay, now that you are all leaving, I feel so low and bad about you all leaving, especially you. Sanay, until today, when you're leaving, I had not realized what and how much you mean to me, now that I'm made obvious that you're moving out of college and that I won't be able to see you every day, I feel so gloomy. I never knew I'm this attached to you Sanay, I don't know what do you think and feel about me, but now, today I've realized that I love you. I feel more than just friendship for you, I today realized that I want to spend more time with you, I actually want to make a 'HAPPILY EVER AFTER WITH YOU'. I've no idea what your response to this will be but I Love you. I hope if you don't love me, you'll at least not end friendship with me, thank you for everything to three of you, especially you, I love you!" Sanay turned speechless reading the letter and doesn't know what to say, but looking at Nabhya being happy knowing he loves her, feels lighter and happier, he says "I love you Nabhya", being extremely happy and emotional, Nabhya says "I love you too, Sanay," the entire movie, all the three love stories impact Nalini like never before, of course the fun moments of movie became enjoyable, but the love stories, especially Advait and Navya's, reminds her of Aadit, she recalls every moment she had spent with Aadit, how amazing she felt with him, the sense of comfort, the sense of safety, but then she breaks down about how things worsened, how they just let go of each other. Sara patiently convinced her, relating to Reyansh's love and Sanay love, she tried explaining how Reyansh and Samitha had a happy family in and arranged marriage, she said "Nalini you might have one such happily ever after like Reyansh and Samitha or you see, love has got another chances, just like Sanay You never know what life has got for you Nalini, get out of what has happened, it's your decision, now try to move on from it, you've come here to begin anew, not to recall Aadit and cry each night" Nalini then calmed herself and a bowl of her favorite Alphanso flavored ice – cream from 'Craving Essentials-36' her favorite ice cream brand or second most favorite for she loved 3-4 flavors from two of her most favorite ice – cream brands, not being able to decide which she loves the most. Anyway the movie ended up reminding her of what she wanted to forget, she finished the ice – cream and recorded her journal, her diary and both the beautiful friends went to bed, turning off the lights and switching on the bed lamp, over 30 minutes adjusting the AC temperatures and the blanket.

A new day is a new start, each day is filled with surprises, for we never know what's coming our way in the next moments, though the day planned it might have changes, destiny might have other plans. Today was one such day at Nalini's baking workshop. As she attended the class that evening, she met a Video Game designer and an enthusiastic baker, speaking to each other Mrs. Sameeksha and Nalini learned that both are in the field of entertainment designing. Mrs. Sameeksha asked Nalini if she's looking forward to work as an Entertainment Designer in a company that Sameeksha's husband owned. Nalini being a thoughtful person agreed to work in there, Mrs. Sameeksha then said, "Nalini, that's good of how active you're shows how much determined you are, despite being into here just since a week you're doing so many things, Anyway this is my husband's card and here is the mail ID to which you're supposed to mail your CV, however, I'll be the one to recommend you, Good luck sweetheart". Nalini smiles and says "Thank you aunty, I'll be grateful to you". She then walks back to apartment by the dusk. As she reaches and freshens up Sara comes by and Nalini with all the excitement tells her about her new beginning and about how she got it. Sara lights in joy for her best friend and wishes her luck and hugs her tight.

The two friends sit straight on the couch and searches about the company, finds out about 'Enigma Edge Studios Co' it being one of the leading animations and video games developer/designer, very thankful for the opportunity, Nalini jumps in joy, and types the mentioned mail ID, attaches her CV and prays to her favourite god for her selection and sends the email. The night becomes a very envisioning one yet a kind of stomach filled with butterflies feeling, for probably the next morning might have a reply. Filled with excitement and a hope of new, Nalini wakes up at 5.00 AM, freshens up, practice yoga and keep waiting for Sara to wake up. The time seems passing too slow as she's been waiting for the reply. After waiting for 7 long hours since 5:00 AM, Nalini received a reply that asked her for a walk in interview the same evening as of what she had to skip her baking class; very happy, very excited, very nervous, she got all dressed for the interview, however she was confident about her previous works and dedication, she was however prepared for the interviews, all ready, she lightened a diya to god, prayed for the best and left to office. Reaching in 15 minutes, she took a deep breathe and entered the office. Greeted a few people working and being assisted of by one reached the cabin. 45 long minutes in the cabin with the MD, and other board members, the interview was smooth enough, impressed by her previous designs the interviewers discussed for about 3 minutes and decided to select her and appoint her, for which they said her "We're impressed by your performance your work and confidence is impressive, we will still discuss about the same and mail you, your results". "Thank you Sir, ma'am, looking forward to serve the best possible and beyond, if I get an opportunity to, Thank you". Nalini smiled and left the cabin. On the way back home Nalini bought her favorite ice-cream for Sara and her, hoping for selection and an offer letter from 'Enigma Edge Studios Co' as she reached, she freshened up and started preparations for dinner. It was 8:15 pm by that time and even Sara reached, as soon as sara reached and rang the bell Nalini opened the door and hugged Sara, and she went like 'Sara, the interviewer said he's impressed by my work, I'm very happy about it hoping that I'll be selected". Sara said, "don't worry darling, you'll for sure be selected, let's pray for the best, All the best my sweety" Then Nalini said Sara to freshen up and until then she'll look some curry and rice, Sara went to freshen up and while moving to kitchen Nalini said "Freshen up soon I've even get some ice-cream for us, let's have dinner and listen to music with ice cream", Sara said okay. By the time Sara freshened up Nalini Cooked and kept the dinner ready to be served. Sara freshened up and came for dinner, the two beauties had dinner, did the dishes and jumped to the couch, chit chatted & giggled for a while, 30 minutes down they played some loveable music and enjoyed every bite of Nalini's favorite ice-cream. Nalini dozed off after finishing her bowl of ice cream, Sara got her a blanket and put it over her, but as Sara turned off the music Nalini woke, and together they got walked to bedroom and turned the lights off, shut their eyes awaiting for a new day.

Sara's sleep woke when the bell rang and a ray of sun fell into their room, she opened the door collected the milk packets, and freshened up. Nalini was into a peaceful sleep after so many nights post her breakup, while she woke as the cycle bell rang while the newspapers were being distributed in their community. She woke and saw the time, it was 6:52 AM, she saw Sara was already up, Nalini then stretched for a few minutes and freshened up, Sara had begun pre – preparations of breakfast while Nalini made some lemon tea for the two. It was 8:26 AM when all the breakfast was ready and the two had it well with some chitchat and Nalini's mail box open. It was 9:00 AM and Sara noticed Nalini's laptop wasn't connected to wi-fi, so did she Connect and refreshed her laptop, Nalini jumped in joy and excitement hugged Sara, cried a bit and called her dad, "Papa, I got the job, I'm selected, I've received the offer letter saying to join from Monday," her dad said "Congratulations Nalini beta," she says "Thank you papa, where's maa?", informing Nalini that her mom's taking Shower the conversation ended, and her dad declined the call. Sara congratulated her said her to reply them with a joining letter. Nalini said "Yeah right help me with that please". "Okay, come" smiled Sara. Nalini and Sara together framed and typed a joining letter and mailed it to the company also took a print out of it and kept the hardcopy in Nalini's handbag. Sara gets ready and leaves for work, Nalini plans to set up her wardrobe. She takes out all the clothes and boxes out of her wardrobe, thinks for around 10 minutes alike every girl about how to arrange her wardrobe. Then she began to sort out different outfits standing around the bed in a messy bun, an oversized tee and a track pant, the perfect cleaning pose-the right hand on waist and left hand on her neck or chin, keeps changing with ideas. After almost 2 hours she arranged her dress, tops, trousers, jeans, tees and some ethnic wear, all of them neatly and according to use. She then lied on bed for a few minutes, then made herself some lime juice with some mint and basil leaves. Then she played some music and continued to set her wardrobe, done with dresses, she took to arrange her skincare and make up, it took her about an hour to sort and neatly arrange her skincare, makeup and accessories separately. Then after all long hour, she took into hands the old cartoon box and began to check each of the things in the box, she found her old penguin plushie that she loved since childhood, it was a serendipity. Then she found her old ceramic coffee mug's handle that broke in a hurry, her favorite coffee mug in a moss green shade with a beautiful ceramic spoon with it, however it was broke, so she only saved the handle of the mug. Nalini has always been a kind of girl that loves keeping memories collected. Looking at the mug's handle her school memories altogether strike, she recalled how hurry it used to be to have a cup of milk early in the morning while leaving for school, she recalled how it was always an incomplete pair of socks the usually delayed her to school about 10 minutes, everything just seemed like yesterday, she smiled and kept it her favorite vintage wooden handcrafted heavy box that had to hold many more of memories. Then she found a few polaroids, one with her dad on her first birthday, her favourite coffee shop polaroid, her favourite restaurant and ice cream parlour, all of it filled her with joy. There were more polaroids tied in a sheet by a satin ribbon, she then found polaroids that she loved, various pictures of her and Aadit together, his family picture, her favourite picture of him and so many pictures of the two kissing, cuddling, she then recalled all of it, the sense of Safety and homely that she only felt when wrapped in his arms, the beautiful sound of his heartfelt that got to be her favorite music to listen everytime, the musky deep fragrance of her perfume that stayed on her almost a day when they embosom or cuddled. She then found herself lost in his husky, deep yet honeyed voice and terribly missed Aadit, she started feeling lovelorned, prior to that she was quite halcyon but looking at the pictures she missed Aadit terribly but already so apart she sighed and continued arranging, keeping his pictures aside safer to journal them in her diary. Then the found her old jhumka, which has been her favourite but she had lost one in some event. She's been a person that cherished memories. Then she found her diary and kept it with the polaroids.

This thing is one of the major differences between men and women. Saying men and women here doesn't mean all the men or all the women, however it is the most of each men and women. Women are more likely to keep memories collected, most of the men generally live it that moment, feel happy, sad or anything as of the matter and usually not journal the memories, however even men have memories that made them feel special they just do not journal each of it, that is how they have been raised.

Nalini continues arranging her wardrobe one by one collecting the souvenirs in her handcrafted victorian box. She found the chocolate wrappers that Aadit used to get for her in the beginning of their relationship, she looked at each one and recalled each meet up, how with so much love he used to get her so many chocolates, the cozy, hugs, the lovely conversations she missed it all ever again, She found a few roses he had given, all dried yet memories so fresh in heart. She couldn't control her tears no more, from a small misunderstanding, an apology to yet another 'I love you' to one another she couldn't let go been a single day of 6 years, She broke down, cried looking at and cherishing each of the things Aadit had presented. She held the roses, pecked them to her eyes filled with tears, took to her hands the dress he had presented to her, she had loved the floral embroidery but now she embossed it to herself broke down, missed Aadit terribly wanting to hug him, see him, hear to his musky deep voice, he always was ineffable to her. She had lionized Aadit so much in her life that every moment of her life she missed him more than she ever missed her family after being to Celestial City. She took the letter from the box, opened it and found Aadit's handwritten love for her, reading each line, with tears filled eyes for each word of love, feeling what might have made him just let her go now, for the same man had written so much love, had written for her how he wants to spend all his life with her and only her, how he didn't want to lose her ever no matter what the situation, each of it felt like a lie for how they just got separated like they were nothing at all, while to her Aadit meant her whole life. Less did she know Aadit loves her more, she too meant all his life to him, but circumstances lead to different decisions for people, no matter how one loves another. She felt like crumbling the paper but each word had settled her heart like the greatest memory, rolling down tears blurred the letter but each memory was so clear enough. Keeping it all aside, she took a picture of him, looked at it for about 7 minutes in tears, despair,love and a very intangible feeling, she felt like 'I need Aadit for the entire life' but a sudden realization, a sense of panic hit her realizing Aadit is no more in her life, Aadit no more loves her. Each thought creating feeling of self doubt, denial and hatred, mis-assuming herself to not have been a perfect partner yet feeling he wasn't so in love with her, crying out for so long, having eyes swollen and legs weak, with an undescribe-able sensation in the stomach and chest, a feeling of love, doubt, acceptance of the separation. She then took some fevicol and journaled each of the polaroid picture of Aadit and both of them together, sticking into her diary the letter he had given,each moment only tears rolling down cheeks in pain and his memories. She each moment felt Aadit will not have faked the loved, he has left because he might have started disliking her, for she believed Aadit genuinely loved her until all the things were seeming like a fairy tale. She wondered how Aadit never told about how he felt, she was confused, yet she cries in deep love.

Crying almost about 3 hours, Nalini felt completely drained. Each and everyday of 6 years striked into her mind, Aadit's memories kept her occupied, it seemed okay in the first few days but as time passed she missed him more than usual.

She wondered what's wrong for generally people move on with time after a break up, but it seemed opposite to her. She always told Aadit "There's no way I will be able to live without you, I cannot imagine a life that doesn't have you with me" Aadit always said "Neither can I live without you, hold me back always, hold onto me, you mean the entire life to me" but she realized he said this only in the initial 6 months of their relationship later always when Nalini said she couldn't live without him or she needs him always Aadit answered like "don't be so emotionally dependent on me", this always consumed Nalini but her emotional attachment to Aadit was so excessive that she was completely involved with him, each day with him was a special day to her, despite arguments, misunderstandings and distances she could never in any moment give up on him. However she consoled herself and freshened up, after setting up her wardrobe as per her regular use. It was 4:00 pm until Nalini freshened up and sat on her cozy chair in the balcony checking a few video game designs and looking for a few fashion designing workshops. Nalini then dresses herself in a Straight-lose fit denim and a blue chiffon kurti, puts on a mild tinted lip gloss and completes with a rosy and cherry fragranced perfume. Not forgetting to accessorise she adds a minimalist chic look of an neck piece that gave her a subtle look and an amazing confidence to walk to her baking class. As she reached the baking class, she greeted Mrs. Sameeksha and thanked her for the amazing opportunity of work. Mrs. Sameeksha congratulated Nalini and wished her luck for the further days at work, and gave her slight hug. For the day Nalini had prepared Aadit 's favorite cheesecake, the workshop was about to end, this was the last week and as per her wish she had learnt to bake Aadit's favourite cheesecake, she felt a sense of happiness, a feeling that was inexpressible, every memory striking, yet feeling better having to learn to bake her favorite person's favorite cake. Being the last week, her workshop had the last one day, as she had completed baking brownies and the major goal of her - Aadit's favourite cheesecake and a basic of few cookies, she had to collect the certificate next evening and bid a goodbye. However it was a good thing, for she had to join to work the coming week. Along her she carried 2 two slices of cheesecake to home for herself and Sara. It being a workshop for an hour and half it was 6:30 pm by when Nalini reached home, by the time even Sara had been home and had freshened up, waiting for Nalini for the evening chit-chat and some coffee. When Nalini reached and said she got for both the Cheesecake she baked, Sara expressed a look of excitement to taste it, however both of them kept it for desserts after dinner. Sara made some coffer until Nalini freshened up and changed her dress. Then both together very comfortably settled in the cozy small Swing-Chair in the balcony. Sara shared how her day at work was and she kept speaking of each moment at office, both of them laughed together out loud. Nalini Spoke about the workshop, she told of how she learnt Cookies, brownies and Aadit's favorite cheesecake. Both together then went to get some veggies for dinner, going by walk in the evening breeze was something Nalini loved, in the nearest super store they got some vegetables, a packet of chips and two packs of blueberry yoghurt, and a packet of biscuit that Nalini took for the stray dog downstairs their community-society apartments Before going home, she fed the dog the biscuits and Sara and Nalini went in, upstairs to their flat. Discussing about what to be cooked for dinner, after 15 minutes they decided to cook some vegetable fried rice. It took 30 minutes for the dinner to be ready to be served, turning the TV on, watching a new series both finished their dinner and did the dishes. Both freshened up and followed their night skin care routine, for about 15 minutes. Then Sara went to the balcony, Nalini got the cheesecake to both and settled in the cozy Swing -chair, Sara took a bite and called it the taste of food in heaven, Nalini was happy to hear it, taking a bite and thanking Sara, Nalini broke down, "I wish Aadit could taste the cheesecake I made, I learnt this because it's his favorite" resting onto Sara's lap and crying her heart out, she calmed while Sara consoled her saying "It's okay Nalini, you gave your best to save you two. And this is why I had asked you not to focus on learning the cheesecake that Aadit likes" Nalini then said "I don't know why, but I can never let go of him, every moment I miss him, I miss how he loved me, I miss the day we first met, the first time he hugged me, actually since then I never felt like leaving him, I always wanted to stay embossed to him, his amazing musky perfume that stayed on me, deep honeyed voice, his lovely hands that I always held, I miss each of it. I miss how he held me and wrapped me in his arms, I miss him so much Sara" Cried Nalini until she couldn't breathe. Sara consoled her, held her and explained her to focus on the further coming job and made her stop crying, wiped her tears and both finished the cheesecake and went to bed, Nalini browsed a few books online for a while found a book 'JUNE' she liked the cover of it and also the title quite different, she ordered it and then dozed off keeping aside the phone. It was however two more days for her to join for work.

Saturday in the morning Sara woke up at 7:00AM, freshened up and made some lemon tea for both, Nalini too woke up by 7:30 Am and together sipped the lemon tea. Both of them nattered a while and planned to go shopping the next day evening. For the Saturday evening all they decided to do was chill at home, making it a sorted cozy evening. Both together practiced some yoga until 8:30 Am, took shower and prepared their breakfast. Getting done with breakfast Sara checked on what does she want to shop and listed it out together with Nalini, next did Nalini, listing few casual, professional outfits, a few hair accessories, some skin care. Passing the time together until it was time for Nalini 's baking workshop, however as the course was finished and she had to only collect the completion certificate, she asked Sara to accompany her, both dressed up and all ready walked the down lane and reached the baking class. Nalini introduced Sara to Mrs. Sameeksha and a few other batchmates. Collecting the certificate and wishing her friends a goodbye Nalini and Sara left. On the way back home two of them got a packet of soup to be cooked for dinner. As they reached home, they changed the dress and started preparing for the dinner. Together finishing the dinner and chores hit the bed, waking the next morning to the early morning bird's chirping and vibrant yet calmer than regular sun rays imposed in the window of their room. Nalini walked to the balcony and loved the trees bristling with potential, breathing the fresh air, viewing a glorious morning she rubbed her hands and gently wiped them all over her face. Sara jazzed up by the time Nalini freshened up, Sara walked to the balcony to witness the glorious morning alike Nalini, by the time Sara freshened up, Nalini made some strawberry milk for the both, enjoying the drink to beautiful morning in the balcony, it was a great beginning to the both friends' Sunday it was seeming like a placid day, indeed it was going to be one, for a soothing start to the day would make whole day a placid Sunday. Done with the douche both of them prepared some poha for the breakfast and finished the breakfast and chores, also pre-preparing some vegetables for the lunch.

On the couch both evoked some memories, nattered about each other's families, friends and college previously. Sara shared how her college life used to be as a student in restoration architecture, very few people being interested into restoration architecture Sara was one, so does she love her work for its been her passion to know about heritage and history and restore the constructions, giving them a life without annihilating the originality of it. Nalini spoke out about how Entertainment designing has been, a very distinctive, thought provoking, enthralling bachelors graduation. Both discussed how days in college have been, in and off campus, friends, experiences and all of it. Both then prepared and had lunch. Freshening up and getting ready both left for shopping around 3:48PM. It is never that shopping gets done in an hour, especially when it's just two best friends. Searching a new fit in each and every outlet surrounding, searching for the perfect pair of denim or trousers for that one top either of them didn't want to leave or searching a perfect top for the trouser they loved, Formal, semi-formal to chic cute pinteresty fits, to choose each kind, to trial, it all and finalise they didn't realize when the clock turned 3:48 PM to 7:15 PM, so did they decide to have dinner at the nearby restaurant and Nalini didn't want to miss her favourite ice-cream. After the bills paid, the two walked to COZENIE restaurant a few hundred meters away from the shopping center. Settling down the tables in any restaurant Celestial City during the weekends is a great task for usually all the tables are reserved, to their luck one table was available, the last one for the evening. Nalini felt more lucky when they were guided to their table which was on the terrace, an open dining, one of the favorite kinds of Nalini, both wondered how is it possible that a terrace table is vacant which had a great city light view both then said anyway its our luck we've got the table on terrace and started checking the menu. Both discussing it's going to be a busy Schedule from tomorrow for the two and both have to go for work came to finalize the order. As the waitperson greeted them with nodding gesture and asked for the order. Sara ordered two mocktails, one for each and a starters, Nalini finalized the main course, making sure they do not fill their hunger the two ordered only a little, for Nalini 's major goal for night was her favorite ice-cream from 'Craving Essentials -36'. Fifteen minutes later they received the food and got it Served. Loving the mocktail and starters both together finished half starters main -course however they had ditched rice for the ice cream. It took 45 minutes for the two to finish the dinner. By the time they paid the bill and reach the exit of the restaurant it was 8:30 Pm. On the way back home they decided to take away the ice-cream tub rather than having it in there. Nalini and Sara ordered their favorite ice-creams in the ice-cream parlour that was a walk of 10 minutes from the restaurant. Carrying the tub of their favorite ice-creams both reached back home by an auto. As they reached and freshened up, they made sure to settle their new dresses in the wardrobe and make sure to have ample space for the new accessories and skin care essentials. All of it took them almost an hour. Then to never miss splashing some water on face before bed both got it done, brought the ice-cream tubs, half covered in blanket, turning on the web series they left at half, together sharing the ice-cream and finishing a few episodes the two friends fell asleep setting an alarm for 6:30 AM the next morning.

Sara's office was a fifteen minutes walk from their home in the North, Nalini's office is the same towards East. Monday morning being a new beginning to Nalini had much of excitement, nervousness and filled with new plans and goals.

Anyhow, no matter what we plan our days like, but destiny will have its own plans for us, who would know it better than Nalini that planned all her future with Aadit but destiny got her to Celestial City which she had never planned of, or thought of.

A new morning, with new start wakes a person, before the alarm rings, same of it happened with Nalini, her eyes were wide open by 6:03 AM, filled in with excitement, nervousness, doubts, and so many more mixed feelings. The fresh air, t few stretches made her quite relaxed: Brushing her teeth took longer than usual for she was dwelled into the thoughts of how today's day at work going to be, how the work will be, how the colleagues will be and so much more to have thoughts of. Realising it'll keep getting late, after brushing her teeth, she moves to kitchen and makes some lemon tea for herself as well as Sara. By the time she make some pre-preparations for their breakfast and lunch that had to be packed, the alarm awakens Sara. Sara wonders why's Nalini already up doing all the work, she asks about it to Nalini to which Nalini explains her mixed feelings about a new start. Sara calms her down and asks her to relax, she says "There's nothing difficult sweetheart, at least not for you, because you love this work and even if there's anything your colleagues will help you out, nobody is going to be a villain, take a chill pill, everything is going to be sweet and to what's not I know you will for sure handle perfectly, better than the way it needs to be handled" and gives Nalini a soothing and hug and moves to freshen up. Until Sara freshens up Nalini Cooks their breakfast. As Sara comes, together the two have breakfast. Then Nalini and Sara cook some vegetable and tortillas for their lunch, done cooking, Nalini moves to take shower while Sara prepares the day's outfit for herself. Nalini then gets ready by time Sara takes shower, after the two getting ready and packing their lunch, Nalini picks up her required files and the two lock the door and bid a bye for work and walk towards their offices. On the way to office Nalini has so many feelings about the first day, about office. She even wondered how unexpected the day is, for she never thought of it or planned it. She had thoughts of how different this morning would have been if Aadit was there, how different work would have been if Aadit was a part of it to know about her life happenings, while she missed Aadit she even wondered or thought about how as an employee she is going to be, what kind of a colleague she going to be? would she be able to give hundred percent to her work? This Monday morning in Nalini's life was a morning alike a new being, alike all us when we're having a new start or like a student's exam? A pilot's flight? Knowing one can do it but still the feeling of nervousness and excitement combined, the kind of feeling that does not have a particular word. The fifteen minute walk to office didn't feel like fifteen minutes. Sighing for the best to happen Nalini stepped into the office for the first day at work. As she goes she receives a warm welcome from her colleagues, then being greeted by her manager, explaining her what's she supposed to get indulged in, how's her team like and who all it is consisting of. Being introduced to her team members, Akshay, Abherr, Saanjh, herself, she learned Abheer is on a week's leave and until he returns the three members need to work on the upcoming projects. She loved how there's no head of group and all of them could be friends in work, however a senior designer would supervise and valuate the projects that the teams work on. But the concept of office was a friendly environment, a great place to work at for a sweet, kind woman like Nalini. Discussing about each other and to know each other better Nalini, Akshay and Saanjh engaged in a conversation for a team to work together needs to be friends like none other and all team of one as a whole. Nalini loves how soft spoken as a woman Saanjh is, Akshay, however Spoke very little throughout, when it was his favourite topic Akshay would turn to be a very informative person, about work, about designs. Saanjh tells Nalini about Abheer being a great co-worker, a very helping person, kind man and an amazing designer, she tells Nalini he's on leave for a week for he's gone to Prithvidur. Nalini wondering it, tells, Saanjh and Akshay that she is from Prithvidur and had come to celestial city for work. And asks if Abheer is from Prithvidur too or has gone with matter of work, Akshay tells he basically is from Prithvidur later maybe now 15 years ago their family shifted away,from there Abheer has joined here for work, now as his father is retired they have shifted back to their native Prithvidur, Abheer has taken leave for the same to make all the settlements an ease to his parents. Nalini then replied "Oh okay. I get it. It'll be good working with you all. Thank you Saanjh and Akshay". Saanjh asks Nalini, where do you live here? With Who? "I've recently moved to Celestial City, I live with Sara, we share a sororal bond. we live at the Ivy wood bay street "answered Nalini in her soft-spoken voice with a gleeful face, and asked where do you both live? Saanjh said she has moved to Celestial City with her sister for work, in her town lives her parents, brother and his wife. Here in Celestial City she and her sister live in Gallery Garden Apartments at the downtown Lofts residential street: Akshay the goes like I live here with my family at Lily Cedars Street, we own a cottage down that lane. I'm working for some experience currently other way round I've different plans and for now however dad is still into business so didn't have to take it over. Nalini nods to both and says nice. Good luck to both of you, on your plans. Both of them thank Nalini and wishes her the same further the three moving to their workspace, both Saanjh and Akshay makes Nalini aware about the ongoing project that began just yesterday and the deadline is a week away. Studying the requirement and challenges Nalini learns about the required design more thoroughly and says her team mates "we'll work on it, the two respond it with a smile and nod. Beginning the work on desk to complete the days desired goal, the three worked well on it until it was 2:00 PM: the time for lunch. Nalini's team and another team together had lunch in the staff cafeteria. Post lunch Saanjh and Nalini got an ice cream, offered it to Akshay but he wasn't an ice cream fan so he denied having ice-cream.

Continuing to work on the design of the story based video game for a client, Nalini enjoyed the design process of the day. It was an ancient themed story based on the hero- superhero in the game had to destroy the level wise monsters, however the suspense lied in the later levels portraying the largest monster being the one that killed the super-hero's father for the sack of precious gems and more treasury. Nalini has always been a tenacious woman towards work, thus her work most of the time was Cynosure. It was already 5:00pm and they hadn't realised it for they were so dwelled into the design. It was when Akshay received a message and checked time when they dismissed the day's work. Bidding a bye to her team Nalini walked towards her home and on the way back she called Sara to ask if she's done yet, Sara also had left office by the time. It was 5:28 PM by the time Nalini reached home, Sara had also just reached and freshened up, as Nalini freshened up the two sipped some coffee by the balcony's swing. Later preparing the dinner and having it, post cleaning the dishes, the two enjoyed the fascinating weather, the Zephyr by the balcony and the twinkling star, they spent almost an hour or even more nattering the day at office; then enjoyed the silent night and Nalini's favorite night sky and the soothing zephyr.

Four Days Later

It was the day of review of the design by Nalini, Saanjh and Akshay, their work was however reviewed and approved by the senior designer, the friday morning it had to signed and approved by the M.D for the afternoon's meeting with the client that proposed for the game. Mrs. Sameeksha's husband, Nalini's employer - Founder of 'Enigma Studios.Co.' was inspired by the design, storyline, and the advanced graphics that gave the game a realistic feeling for the player. The team was appreciated and the meeting was allotted at 2:15pm, totally an obstruction to the lunch time. It was 2:00 Pm until the three revise the presentations, charts and their strong reasons for the storyline selection and creation, their reasons for creation of particular characters and the various levels and their variation of difficulties with proper reason for each. Well groomed team, with properly revised presentation the three looked well prepared, confident and extremely dwelled into professionalism, leaving no room of negligence or unethical attitude and body language. With no compromise time the meeting begun at 2:15 pm in the all set conference hall. Nalini was a bit nervous as it was her first project, however Akshay and Saanjh didn't let her down, they encouraged her for the presentation and Akshay made it up for her explaining to keep herself very casual yet professional he conveyed her that she shall assume the meeting is only between their team and she's presenting it only to Akshay and Saanjh. Somewhat better and less nervous Nalini was ready for it, one moving before all the team, clients and senior designers she looked at Saanjh and Akshay, Saanjh held her hand and encouraged her, Akshay gave it a cool smile conveying a thumbs up: you can do it. As she moved before all and introduced herself she kept looking at only Saanjh and Akshay, Akshay directed her to maintain eye contacts with clients more often and conveyed to her that she shall move her eyes to each person seated. Characters, the design theme, the players role, graphics and handed over the further to Akshay, Akshay and Saanjh were super proud of Nalini's presentation, her convincing approach, her language, her soft-spoken yet bold explanation to each part of design. Mrs. Sameeksha's husband, the clients and senior designers were impressed of her work and the presentation, for the way she presented and conveyed each bit was a very unique approach with very convincing style. Akshay and Saanjh done with the presentation in the best way alike always for each project previously sighed a relief of completion with a smile of satisfaction on the both's face. Saanjh hugged Nalini and expressed that she's super proud of her work, Akshay gave a friendly hug on the side and said how proud he felt of Nalini on her first and best presentation. She felt so happy and satisfied about her work and thanked the two. Later she received a token of appreciation from her senior designer as well as Mrs. Sameeksha's husband. It was a great day at work for Nalini. As soon as she returned home she nattered it all to Sara in joy. And then as she freshened up, sipped up Coffee, both engaged in the dinner preparation, post dinner they enjoyed cool breeze in balcony, listened to a few songs and dwelled into a great sleep under the soft hug of blankets, knowing there's no hurry of office for the next two days, of course there's no special weekend plans but the night that has no hurry for the next morning is a very satisfying one, for Nalini or all of us.

Saturday morning begun with a strawberry milkshake and the day passed on with some movie hours, an evening walk and some chit chatting. Nalini received the book 'JUNE' that she had ordered. She loved how the cover of the book had been designed, a choice of vibrant design and sober colour theme, bold yet attractive minimalistic design. Nalini has always been deeply interested in human psychology, reading the introduction she was beyond satisfied to know that the book involved psychological facts about humans. Her keen interest to know about human emotions, feelings and psychology developed in her late teens, however it was her interest since early teenage but as she grew older she developed interest to study about it, but she had not been into any major decisions on it. However, she was glad to have received the book during weekend as she could calmly focus a little more, the fact that the book was even about a little human feelings, especially men, she developed more interest to read it thoroughly and understand it deeper.

As she finished the introduction, she checked the table of contents that included:

- How men and women are different psychologically?

- What made men and women the way they are today?
- Differences in men and women's reaction to different circumstances.
- Men in love
- Role of man: Son, Brother, Husband, Father
- Men at work and for Society.
- How are men understood or misunderstood.

Nalini loved how different the book stands out of others. She shares the same with Sara and expresses how amazing of a book this might be as it stands out on a very less cared topic.

The book conveyed, "This book does not intend to anyway convey against women nor does it anywhere mean 'All men', but it tries to convey about a very general aspect about most of the boys or men. The content of the book does not mean to convey that women are at all ease or women are the cause of men's difficulties, it only aims to convey the very long period's concept about men and their emotions. Never meaning women are less at any work or women seek attention, at least not all women. Author accepts women are unsafe at the current situations of increasing rapes, abuses or any kind of harm or discomfort that women face, thus clearly mentioned, whatever the book conveys in favour of any gender it does not mean 'All the people of gender', i.e 'ALL MEN' nor 'ALL WOMEN', for its most of the men, raised the way or the societal image of how a man is supposed to be. At the end, 'Not all men are good men, not all men are goons or rapists; Not all women are attention seekers, not all women are angelic. In any aspect, its neither all men nor all women, GOOD or BAD, it's not the gender, its the individual". Nalini loved how deep the message is, how sensitive it is and she knew the book would be a great read, to anyone, a man or a woman. As she moved to the next page and read about:

How Men and Women Are Different Psychologically

It is very well known that men and women are physically very much different. To a lesser known fact is that men and women are mentally and psychologically even more differently built. Hormones being one of the most major element that makes the two gender so different from one another. It is from the time of birth, moving to puberty and to adulthood how hormones play a role in the behaviors of men and women.

Typically as we define a perfect man is who is more physically strong, it is purely about the testosterone. Increase in the testosterone levels increase physical strength and aggression behavior.

There is a lot of difference between choices of men and women. Men are more likely to choose machineries and gadgets whereas women are more likely to choose good relations over other things. Men are more logical thinkers whereas women dwell into emotions in all that they do. Females choose beauty, men choose intelligency, which makes a lot of differences between the two.

Psychologically men are more logical and work in silence. Still women have the highest form of intelligence: INTUTION, which is 80 percent of the time exactly what their intution has been. Men posses a logical perspective to every happening where as women take all of it personally and emotionally.

Women have a great verbal ability and freedom whereas men do not have that. This is purely on how the individual has been raised. Typically as boys are prepared to be strong, that boys do not cry, boys can deal with it all independently, boys have to posses the quality of anger, dominance, if not he's less likely a man, for if he does not show anger or isn't dominant or is emotionally involved into someone or something than professional about it, if a man is soft and sober he's labelled to posses feminine energy where as he is just a normal man with more emotional intelligence, less of aggression or is soft spoken with a honeyed voice.

All boys being raised to be a "MAN" is what snatches their freedom of expressing emotions which later comes from him: "It just cannot be expressed in words" where as it is just that they cannot, they do not have the ability to express their feelings verbally for that is how they are raised - "To Be a Man' by meaning, 'not to cry like a girl', not to complain', to be strong- meaning let your emotions stay within you, very casually being told, these sentences build a loving boy to a man: A man that is now being called Emotionless or Cold hearted, but it is never realised that he's built that way, if otherwise he's labelled to posses more feminine qualities.

A small boy is asked to stop crying like a girl when he stumbles or falls and cries in pain, it since then a 6 year old boy is asked to Man Up.

A 17 year old is asked to be a 'cool guy' and not an emotionally invested boy, since then it is when he's been built to be not expressive or just not care.

As responsibilities burden the shoulder, it is since then when a man is asked to be selfless, impartial yet expected to love each one more than the other.

women's insecurity leads a man to a lot of inconvenient situations, but nowhere women can be blamed for the same as women are built with more attention and care, it is a natural behaviour for every mother and sister to be insecure about a man to be more dwelled into his wife and leave behind how much has his mother invested love, care, affection and every bit of her life for her son, how much a sister has helped, and stood by him since day one. But it is then when his wife feels neglected. Playing all the roles impartially is what 'MEN' have to master at, and this is how almost every emotion of a man is mostly not been taken into consideration, for a mother argues she's known him more, a sister confronts they've known one another deeper and wives confronts she's his better half, she loves him more and knows him much better; where as neither of the three will ever know or understand him completely, it is not a competition, he is a human just like women, but with lesser ability and freedom of expression of his feelings, with higher testosterone making him physically bigger, emotionally more agressive, more logical thinker than emotionally invested. Each of the character in a man is how he's built asking to 'MAN UP' and not hear him emotionally for only believing a man is who is strong, profit oriented, impartial and someone who cannot cry (mostly).

What Made Men and Women How they are Today?

EVERY INDIVIDUAL TODAY IS UNIQUE, DIFFERENT IN A WAY UN-SIMILAR TO ANY OTHER.

There is a different reason for why each person is how he or she today is. Reasons vary individual to individual, it can be childhood trauma, societal expectations, how he/she has been raised, friendships experienced, relationships, the kind of marriage their parents have, and so much more. Reasons are as deep as oceans, one cannot easily come to conclusion on how deep oceans are, what actually the reason is, for how one is today.

People, in life go through so many types of situations, different friends, different family members, losing loved ones by death, being betrayed, not being loved, overly- possessed, failures, successes, achievements, profits or losses, and no person can be judged by just one such situation. The repetition of similar pattern of certain circumstances might affect the person in a particular way, which is what makes the person a certain way.

For instance, women and men are raised very differently each, in Indian families. Since childhood, women are raised and being told about they are quite soft and emotional. While men that do not be dominant, men who do not posses quality of aggression are considered feminine. Women that are certainly short tempered are labelled to be manly and not a proper feminine energy possessing woman. It Is even hormones for why are men and women how they are.

The idea of independent woman does not actually mean what women or most of the people have today assumed it to be. Men and women are both dependent on each other in atleast one or the other way. Men and women are biologically so very different and that is how they are created to be, which even makes them psychologically different, which no matter what financial independence either gender attains, it is a fact to be accepted that both women and men are inter-dependent. It just cannot make women and men live without one another just because both of them earn more than enough to live, to buy all that they'd like to have, it is more than just money and luxury, it is being cared, caressed, loved, understood, companionship is quite a necessity. A lot of people today might find it bullshit that being told about Companionship but deeper in life money can buy us a house but only a family can make it a home, money can buy us clothes but a compliment from favorite person would make the outfit more charming, money could buy us food but the food cooked with love would make it tastier. Money will buy us a luxurious car but at least after 50 Solo trips we'd need someone to travel with... Money will buy us everything but nothing of that will be something like love.

Today women are misunderstood to be attention seeker's and men as play-boys or cold-hearted. Quite true to what some of us will have gone through, but not every woman would be an attention seeker nor will every man be a play boy, rapist or always a cold hearted. It is since birth how women are given excess attention what might today make women wanted to be heard seen, listened to, prioritized which men ultimately would call it seeking attention, for that isn't how they are being raised. Similarly, it is since childhood how boys are asked to MAN-UP, not to cry like "girl", and that is what today most men might be how they mask up to not feed low about a lot of things- for it is very obvious that as humans, we all feel happy/sad, and it & quite an impossible thing that men far would not be hurt. It is just the way how typically boys are meant/asked to be stronger, not to cry or it is like a girl; they are raised to be dominant it is what night today men might be "Cold-hearted" or "Care-less about emotional expressions", that is the what we generally see today, men barely express how they feel, and then they be called "EMOTION-LESS" where it is in the roots of being raised, the society.

It does not mean to say all men or all women, it is just most men and most women for the society is how it is.Truly we do not live by society it is how we'd want to, it is just we that matter and not what society thinks but a very much reality is that men and women go hand in hand no matter how much financially the each earn, no matter how much strong one is, both cannot be equal in a lot of terms, men cannot be what women are, women cannot be what men are,if one is the heart of the of home, another is the eye? Basically both men and women are perfectly imperfect, one another completing each other.

Women are disillusioned by relationship changes when men are disoriented by job career changes. Women and men both face midlife crisis, being various reasons, it can be loss of loved one, depression, childhood or teenage trauma, failures, losses or not being able to attain family, work or relationship goals, for being mistreated. Men and women can both have a mid-life crisis, reasons might vary for generally men's dissatisfaction or depression is most of the time their career and women usually are more worried about love, relationships and family, as per a psychological study it is said so, but; anyhow it can be in a few circumstances that men too get depressed in case of a unhappy relationship and even women might face issues like depression if not being able to attain the career goal. Both men and women fell depressed either it is an unhappy, relationship or a dis-satisfied job or career Whatever men and women are today is all depending on what each individual have been through, just that women are expressive about their feelings and men are not so verbally expressive as women, here again neither all men nor all women, but of the both, for women usually are given a ear, a shoulder, but when it comes to men they are expected and built to be epitome of strength, emotionally as well, not knowing crying or speaking out how he feels is not weakness but a need, for if he puts out his feelings he could feel much better, the burden of all of it when bursts in aggression or anger will his might have irreversible situations where as if the he speaks out or tries to feel lighter, situations might be better than how they turn to be when his unexpressed feelings becomes aggression, uncaring.

Differences in Men's and Women's Reaction to Different Circumstances

It is well known that most commonly everyone believes men are more logical thinkers and women are more emotionally involved into the situations they deal with. There is a lot of difference in how men deal with things, and how women do it, there are a lot of things that men find it easy to deal with and on the other side are a lot of things, that women find easy to tackle neither of the two are weak or strong, both are masters in different things that the other one might be average in.

For instance if we consider a relationship, in any argument the male partner comes up with logical or practical things where as a female partner dwells into only emotional reasonings, none of them can be wrong, for a few things require solutions, and the other things require some emotional support. A woman feels loved when her partner listens to her, emotionally supports her or hugs her rather than giving a logical solution to what she's speaking, where as a man will be in search of a practical solution rather than being hugged in such situations/being just emotional.

While men seek for solutions, women need her to heard, taken care of, a lot of such differences make men and women so very different from one another in almost every aspect. As an individual the opposite gender has to understand what their partner needs, One cannot expect his/her partner to feel better by the things he/she does. For example, a man cannot give up because his partner is not satisfied by his logical solutions she needs emotional support, she needs to be understood, instead of giving solutions if he calmly listens to her she'd feel much better; in the same way a women cannot blame a man if he's not satisfied by her comforting words and emotional support for all that he'll be in search of is some proper solution.

This does not mean women aren't capable of solving things or that men aren't emotionally involved in things, it is totally wrong to believe so. Women can of course solve things and men are equally or more involved emotionally into a few things. It is just that women first put out all there emotions and then go on to find a solution where as men being not So verbally expressible, being inexpressible about how they feel for that is how they're built, they just focus on solutions, power and achievements.

Anytime a man is asked about how he feels barely any answer we'd receive but if not all women, but at least 80% of women would feel free to express it through words. Most of the men say its inexpressible, there's no words to say on it' but its just that they are not verbally expressible about things except official things. Most the men are more of the intellectual whereas most of the women are emotional, both being beautiful in the way they are. Both men and women are unique in every way, they're how they've me been built, all it takes for both is to understand each other.

Most of the men are being misunderstood as impatient, short-tempered, aggressive; but most of the time it is their bottled up feelings that come out as anger, like women can cry most men since Childhood are raised in misbelief that men do not cry, 'men are supposed to be strong' whereas men need to express how they feel otherwise they might be involved in addictions like alcohol, they being bottled up for very long period of time can effect them internally, or mentally. Excessive aggression or temper effects their Blood-pressure, there are a lot of men such possibilities as men are badly given a ear to hear.

Anyhow it is hot just a single person, its a whole as a society that is responsible for such misbeliefs about crying is a weakness or that men are only supposed to be strong all the time

Men in Love

Most of the times it is said that 'love is the most beautiful feeling', but love is quite a inexpressible feelings. Love is not just what a teenage couple believe it to be, neither love is what an old age couple portray as love just doesn't bloom, it comes in stages, first being attraction.

Love not includes only romance, it is a responsibility. In a seriously involved relationship, men are more responsible partners while women are more romantic, women are more at the helm about relationship's well being. Women love and dream of a future, whereas men mostly build it, men are power to love and women are light, even if the either isn't invested the relationship shatters. Both men and women should go hand in hand to keep the relationship on track. Love is about faithfulness, a long lived relationship is not just intimacy, it is understanding, discomfort, trust and more.

A study by Johan Alan Lee claimed that men are inclined towards playful love, whereas women are more towards pragmatic love. However, the love experience varies across. Cultures and the individual.

As the factor of age was taken into consideration, it was found that amongst the young respondents the romantic love style was dominant, in the higher age groups companionship,pragmatic love was more common. However just because the study claims, it cannot be considered that all the men opt ludic love/Playful love and all the women are into relationships with all faithfulness, it can be vice-versa as well.

When a man falls in love, he generally brings out his possessiveness to scene... at times a man becomes extremely possessive about his partner, depending on his partner his relationship will change as a reaction of his possession, but to be known is that a man is possessive only when he loves genuinely, nevertheless, not all possessive men are loyal:

A love relationship can result in happiness, peace, a better life marriage; however it might even have marriage Some discomfort and misunderstandings, one just needs to know if its worth it, if the person et genuine, otherwise it can lead to stress, pain, negative feelings. A man in love is the most beautiful creature in the world, for he is someone who becomes the most adorable in all ways, he takes care, he loves, he understands, he protects, a man in love is not someone of who just speaks but is someone who acts the way he says, someone whose actions really show his love, some who prioritizes rather than Just saying he loves her. However, it is the same about a woman in love, it is her actions and not just words, however women are more expressive verbally than men.

Nalini felt way too inexpressible after reading all of it. Her thoughts, her feelings, her ideas, all of it seemed to change drastically. Dwelled deeply into thoughts about what the so far read, she co-related to Aadit, how he might do things, how he'd manage all of it impartially. She felt his anger also might be a a reason of his suppression, his bottled up emotions, she sighed it all and closed her eyes as she turned the lamp off. The next morning, as she had to go to office, she woke up, freshened up, made some lemon-tea for both sara and herself. All aligned, together they cooked some breakfast and packed some lunch. It was by 9:35 AM when two got ready left the for office. As Nalini reached office she received a call from Sara saying she had to leave to her home as her brother met with an accident and is being admitted, Nalini consoles Sara and gives her some strength on tall and wishes her a safe journey. As she moves to her desk, she greets Saanjh and Akshay and takes her seat. Abheer looks at Nalini in complete shock, as he reaches their table, Saanjh and Akshay introduce Abheer and Nalini, they greet each other, with a smile, yet Abheer seems to be shocked to see Nalini.The whole time Abheer seemed shocked sand confused, then decided to directly speak to Nalini about his confusion. At the time of lunch Abheer approaches Nalini and asks her where's she from, as she says Prithividhur, his confusion takes a way towards Surety, he then with no second thoughts asks her if she's the Nalini, Aadit's girlfriend Nalini, the question stunned her. In complete shock Nalini asks Abheer, who are you and what's up? What are you talking to me about? Abheer says her "Relax Nalini, I'm Aadit's childhood friend, we've been best friends since we were 5. When I was about 15 or 17 we moved to a different city, I lost contact to Abheer and never met him for

8 years till the last week. As, my parents Shifted back to Prithvidur, I had been there, it is then when I got to meet Aadit again, he there spoke to me about you for the first time. We had spent a few hours together, then I learnt about your relationship and breakup. Nalini, not because Aadit is my close friend, but he genuinely is a very great man. I know he's a lot inexpressive, a little short tempered but to people he love the most he'd give his life for them. Nalini and he spoke I realized you're one of them in his life. I'm 100 percent sure he'd not have told this to you he might have been aggressive towards you, but Nalini he does that because he always want to portray himself as a strong man, a man who doesn't care but his not so, he cares deeply, his care and concern comes out as over-possession, he portrays like nothing matters to him as of what a 'lot of people assume him to be egoistic, whereas, Aadit is the most kind hearted, down to earth, soft person as far as I've seen". Nalini says "That's great of your friend. See you" and leaves the place. Abheer anyhow just wanted to get the two back together as he had met Aadit and knew he loves Nalini limitlessly. Abheer wonders, how might have the two parted ways. However, he finishes lunch and continues to work. Nalini feels a bit disturbed about what happened

she worries if Aadit really loves her so much like Abheer said, but she wonders why he has been quite arrogant, egoistic towards her, she feels confused if he really it So or she misunderstood him, but she was quite rigid about the spiration, for she needed a emotional understanding, to be loved softly, she needed no ego between the two but she always felt insecure about these things with Aadit, for he was a very inexpressive man, rigid, pretending to be uncareful about things like love.

It was the time to leave for home, Nalini waved a bye to Akshay Abheer and Saanjh and walked back home. As she reached home she called Sara to ask about her brother, but Sara couldn't take call, so Nalini just dropped a message conveying 'I hope you reached safe. Don't worry Sachit will be alright. Call me when you are free, take care', keeping phone aside she freshens up and makes some coffee for herself. Taking the coffee she moved to the Swing in balcony, as she sipped the first sip she was dwelled into thoughts of what Abheer spoke to her. She hadn't realized a cup of coffee took her 30 minutes to finish for all she was thinking of was does Aadit still love her? Is he really how Abheer told or its true that Aadit is egoistic and doesn't care? If he loved me, he'd have not let me go or he at least should try contacting me if he was really what Abheer told, Nalini was just dwelled into thoughts of Aadit. She was in no mood to cook dinner, she listened to a few songs and decided to sleep, but she was quite hungry. She ordered a sandwich and a mojito, had half the sandwich and mojito and hit the bed lugging into blankets, warm s-cozy, however she couldn't sleep soon for she was quite disturbed.

On the other side Abheer spoke to Aadit about Nalini. He had called Aadit to say Nalini and he are working at the same place, and they spoke today. Aadit's tone of talk was very much understandable to Abheer that Aadit misses Nalini a lot, still loves her. However Abheer tried to convey Aadit that he has to try contacting Nalini, but Aadit Said No Abheer, maybe she's not happy with me, I might not be the right one for her, her choices of a relationship might not match mine. I'm a bit aggressive, she's too sensitive, to her everything about me becomes very important so she herself assumes she's not important to one and moreover if she wanted me she'd have not stayed away from me this long" sighed Aadit. Abheer was silent on it, yet a moment later added "I don't think so its something like what you've assumed, it might be both of your ego,if not any inconvenience in relationship are just one deep, clear conversation away from reality and understanding. If you two let your egos win, you both will lose the person you two loved the most?

Aadit however silently put away the topic and spoke of business. As the call indeed, Aadit felt like texting Nalini but he stepped back from doing it.

Nalini couldn't sleep well, she was up again from sleep at midnight 1:23Am, she couldn't sleep despite trying for long. She then woke up, checked the fridge for some ice cream and grabbed it, she then moved to bedroom, opened "JUNE" to continue reading it while having some ice cream.

Men at Work and for Society

Very widely believed about men is that they're more efficient at work than women, technically they 're, but it totally depends on the individual about how much can he work and how much he is capable of. However, every man at work is someone who is focused on achievements. As a society, it generally is pressurized that men need to work and feed a family, however since the past few decades it is quite changed, both men and women work for the family, both are almost equal at work, nevertheless in some corners, at some villages, wages still are higher for men than for woman.

Over all the years, equality has changed for men and women. Both go hand in hand, economically being equal, responsible. As compared to women, men mostly work almost without ego of being independent financially, however women in a few cases misuse the financial independence, similarly to men, again without considering the whole gender it depends on the individual. At times it had happened to believe that as women earn, quite a bit they build in themselves a sense of ego, for which is what a few people feels like women when earn change in terms of a relationship, quite a little believed by some people that women earning at times starts believing of considering she can deal with every happening all by herself, which is quite impractical, here it is not all women, but only a very few. It however depends on individual and not the whole gender.

One needs to understand what equality actually is. When it is said about equality between men and women it might include financial equality: Both men and women can earn equally with no biases on gender.

Intellectual ability: Both men and women can be equally intelligent and capable of working in all the sectors.

What it means is, men and women's equality is upto financial, capability, intelligence; women and men are both psychologically and biologically physical power of a man, or doesn't mean men to have the a emotional intelligence or expressive capacity of a women be physical. Equality cannot be physical a man protects a women physically, he's stronger a woman takes care of a man in a way he can never-it can be spiritually, emotionally,if a man is the strength, a woman the source; he provides, she protects; partes, he's the power of the house, she's the heart; he builds an amazing house, she makes it a home; both men and women are equal in very widely different contexts, both are independent yet inter dependent, they can earn equally yet they need each other for their wealth cannot pay for health but their companionship and love can.

Men are more focused on achievements, they're goal oriented, whereas women are more focused on relationships however they manage both work and family like a magic. Society considers men as providers, society imagines man to have super powers to be impartial, successful, emotionally strong, and much more, very rarely we get to see where men's emotions are given attention to, for it is nobody's fault because that is what have been practiced since ages. For instance, everyone speaks about women's post partum depression, for in reality, men too go through the same,this is studied in psychology, yet way too much ignored, for sure women go through severe pains during Pregnancy and while giving birth, whereas it is totally ignored about man, how he feels after his child is been born, and so much more, a father, a husband, a son, a brother, all of it, all at ones. Very true it is the same for a woman, yet for instance a woman can be partial towards only her child and husband, but a man will be not fine with it, for it is he who will have to make it for his mother, wife, children, etc.

Men are objective driven, women are emotions driven, men's conversations are almost all of the times about their goals, their dream job/ business, cars, etc. while women take about how they feel, and no its not all men and women, and even those who do it aren't wrong, for men and women is that's how they're built, that is how men lose woman that they love, for as they know she loves him, she is he's they stop putting in efforts and the woman is taken for granted, but it is when the woman starts feeling unloved and she parts ways; that is what men need to know, women and their achievement, but woman need constant love, she need to be treated like she is loved and not just for words. At the same time, women need to know men focusing to achieve more doesn't mean he doesn't love her, for a man in love, does all of the thing in the plan of future with her, it has to be a two way understanding and not an assumption or label for the either.

Nalini felt confused about it, what is it about men and women? Are all men egoistic or they're just misunderstood like that for their actions? She missed Aadit a little more, she worried if she misunderstood him? For instance she felt, no, he's weird the next moment she felt he loves me he just cannot express it. Too many such thoughts lift her confused in every way. A moment her love for Aadit made he want them together, next moment she felt he might be better off without her, if not he'd have contacted her. Some moment she felt naive the other in second she neglected it. However, she felt "how Aadit would deal with all of it, he is not so expressive, he has to take care of his mom, brother with all the work load, and even I've walked away from him, how he might deal with it all? "She thought, she terribly missed him, but she couldn't text him, for she feared if he doesn't care at all, for if he did he'd have contacted. It was like, the love failed and ego won kind of situation between the two. Nalini continued to read, as she flipped a page, she fell into sleep, keeping the book open upside down, the table lamp turned on, the warm blanket covering her half.

She in the middle of night- almost morning woke up to a dream, in the dream, it was Aadit. She dreamt of Aadit being alone through all of it, losing his father, taking up all the business, taking care of his family. It was a moment of panic to her. She felt disguised without Aadit, she wanted to see him the same moment, but it was a highly impossible thing. She cried out, confused, in despair, in love but away from loved one. She turned off the light, scrolled a few pictures of Aadit, listening to songs that were quite special to both. Tears rolling down the eyes, his pictures, their pictures together were uncountable, an endless scrolling, she dozed in the middle of it. It was 6:23 Am when the glare of sun and chirp of birds awakened her, it was a new morning, yet a weird feeling, crying for very long the last night she felt a different type of way as she woke up. She went to the balcony, the morning was fresh, yet she was feeling a weird way, tears were only rolling down and she couldn't stop crying, Aadit has been someone she had fallen in love with more than she ever loved her parents too.

However as she had to freshen up, she relaxed herself and freshened up, made some milkshake for herself and again moved to balcony, she was in no mood to cook any breakfast or lunch, she only wanted to spend time all alone, drinking the milkshake, re-reading Aadit's and her texts she again teared all long for an hour and thirty-minutes, then she took shower and got ready for work. As she walked by the streets towards office, she prepared herself to not shed a tear throughout the office hours. As she reached office, she greeted her team-mates alike everyday. Abheer and Nalini were together assigned a little work for the day, Abheer while working noticed Nalini being dull compared to the previous days, she questioned her if something's wrong, she denied it and continued working, though she said nothing, her disinterested attitude towards work, un-involvement made it obvious to Abheer about her disturbance; Abheer then said her, "I know you're upset about Aadit, Nalini, let me tell you, please don't stop me, Aadit has always been a gentleman, after he lost his dad, he completely changed, he was filled up with responsibilities and duties, I don't know if he expressed it you or not, but I've seen Abheer grow from a naughty boy to an amazing man, I have no idea when you guys fell in love, but as I recently spoke to him when I've been to Prithvidur, it was the first time I had seem him so low voiced, short-tempered, he never expresses his feelings but he just turns upside down via his gestures and behavior. As I spoke to him, he mentioned about you, as I asked him who's that and what happened, he went like, Nalini and showed me picture of you, she's who I love so much, words cannot explain that, I don't know if I'm not fine or it just didn't work out, or if she's not happy with me, a lot of arguments, misunderstandings and stuff, I too couldn't stop her I don't know how why and all, but yes she just walked away and I never contacted her, usually she used text me in hardly few hours but this time she left me and never came back, I feel vain, my love, my everything has drained. She was a kind of perfect but maybe it wasn't meant to be, but I do still love her, Aadit told me so much about something for the first time, and I'm sure he will have made this affect him every way, he just doesn't show that up. Nalini, Aadit is different man, if he wanted to leave you he'd have done that long back, he has so much in life, you already know that, don't let both of your egos take you so apart that you can never have each other. Men are inexpressive Nalini, they just choose to let go things rather than speaking up, they need love, the need to be cared, but they end up to be always hearing and never be heard or understood, Aadit needs you, Nalini, don't give up on your love like it means nothing at all, he's just been misunderstood rather wise he loves you beyond anyone else, think of it" said Abheer. Nalini was completely silent throughout, it was the lunch time, Nalini wasn't in any mood for food, she just needed to be alone, she moved to the gardens of office, and scrolled social media for a while, she then thought of continue reading, moving to the next part, Nalini turned the page and read,

Role of Man: Son, Brother, Husband, Father

A boy, since child-hood will be raised to be a strong man, and that isn't something unknown to almost all of us, been asked to man-up every time he cries, or becomes expressive/emotional, this never mean to say that all the women out there are able to express all their feelings/emotions or women's life's easier, but generally men are expected to be emotionally strong- misunderstanding the meaning of emotionally strong as someone that doesn't speak out his heart or doesn't cry, where as one who express how he feels and cries his heart out is many times stronger than a person – man/woman who bottles up everything, as bottling up everything can turn a person to a weak, depressed person or a very aggressive/short-tempered person, which isn't healthy for himself, his surroundings, his relationships.

As a boy in his childhood is usually asked not to cry is made into a teen that becomes quite arrogant, inexpressive which is why in most relationships men are labelled to be emotionally unavailable, uncaring; neither women nor men can be blamed for this thing, for it is collectively all of us responsible for this, even today at few parts of the world maybe, we quite don't find it acceptable when a man breaks down but the other way round is completely fine; however being judgmental has become easier than understanding the opposite person and accepting things.

Not every time, but most of the times, it is obviously spoken how difficult it is as a woman in her life to deal with a lot of happenings and is a very acceptable thing to be spoken about, for as a woman works at home and work-place, woman in love are most of the times are being hurt, left, which is quite difficult for a woman to deal with for she will have invested all of herself for the man she loves, but as a few psychological studies men prefer ludic (playful) love and women mostly prefer emotional love; this however doesn't mean all men choose to only have a playful relationship. One of the most difficult things in a woman's life is believed to be her marriage, for she has to move to a completely new place, live with new people, take care of the new family like her own, treat her in-laws like her own parents even if she's not treated like their daughter, absolutely has to be a difficult phase in each and every woman's life, but to just give a thought about the same with men, a man as he marries will have so many roles to play completely impartially, and even when he does it in the most impartial way, there's his family, his own parents that misunderstand at least ones, at least for a few minutes, his wife that feels he's biased towards his parents, when a woman finds it so difficult when her in-laws misunderstand her, how'd a man feel to be misunderstood by his own parents, his own family; however it is not meant to say that it is easier for a woman but what it actually means is a man is usually misunderstood by his own family and yet expected to be impartial and there is no way anyone can be blamed for the same, for a man will be a mother's son who he has grown up loving him beyond the world, a man will be a sister/brother's sibling who he has grown up with, sharing every bit of life, his wife who has moved to a completely new world where all that she knows better is her husband, who she makes her world, loves beyond herself and the whole world; and there's nobody he can replace for the other, yet each one feels insecure about the other and it cannot be denied as it is the most natural happening, for neither a mother or a sibling would like to e left out nor wife; that is where how a man has to play very diplomatically, impartially. However sometimes even when he does it, he is misunderstood by at least one of the member, and in that case he is labelled to be a lot of things like 'mumma's boy' or 'uxorious' and that is when a man is all drained, loving all of them impartially, yet being misunderstood by his own people, his mom that he loves beyond his life, his siblings that he'd give his life for, his wife that he'd fight the world for. Just like women, it is difficult for men as well, for he is not only misunderstood by his in-laws alike his wife, but he is misunderstood by his parents, the family he grew up with, his wife, his in-laws, for the either way he does, the other person starts feeling neglected, uncared, left-out, where as a man would never mean to leave behind anyone, neither his parents nor his wife; quite naturally a mother is insecure as well as a life – partner, and while each one expects him to be impartial, secretly the each one wants to be loved more, prioritized more, and it is neither of their fault, for a mother will have been there since the birth so she naturally is insecure about a new comer; but a wife is someone that has left behind her whole world and came into a completely new place, among very new people and all of it by trusting her husband, her companion, so naturally she does expect him to be more her's; but a man, in this case have to play roles so impartially that in the process he just sacrifices himself so many times in order to make sure none of them is left uncared or none of them is hurt in any ways.

As Nalini's office resumed after work she folded the corner of the page and moved back to her table, however throughout she was only thinking of Aadit, about how things changed or where they went wrong, reading the book, knowing more about men, she wondered if Aadit also is going through these misunderstandings, if even he's being misunderstood. She wanted to text him, but she even didn't want to be hurt again. As the office timing was over, she waved a bye to her team – mates and walked back to their apartment. As she came and freshened up she made for herself some coffee and moved to swing in the balcony to continue reading from where she left and began –

A man's responsibilities and roles grow when he becomes a father, alike women becoming mother, as a father, a man will have to become a so very different man as a father, for he has to become more selfless, more responsible. Just like women, men too go through post – partum depression and it has always gone unnoticed, very much known how difficult for a woman it is to go through 9 months of pregnancy, the pain, the mood swings, the medical difficulties, the psychological and hormonal changes, but about men it is so unnoticed that barely someone knows about men's post – partum depression, how they feel, what they go through in that phase and how long does it go. Just like motherhood has been described always, fatherhood holds so many of the things too. A boy that had been raised to MAN – UP, being a boy that was only playful, now is a man that is having to be impartial taking care of more than 3 people all at ones making sure none of them feels away/apart, a boy that got everything he asked for is now a man that has come a long way from his needs, sacrificing all of himself for a life that he's got lie from, for a life that has changed her life for, for a life that he has given birth to.

No matter how a man or a woman is, both are judged, a woman is judged differently than a man, but the society is more judgmental than being cheerful for how people come through various things and try to bring the best out of themselves. Men are expected to gain so much, women lose so much throughout, masculinity is judged, femineity is judged, but only the one sailing the boat knows how strong the waves are.

Nalini missed her dad reading the above, she missed Aadit, if even he has to go through all of it. She looked at his pictures, opened his contact to text him but she stepped back. However, she continued reading –

How Men and Women React When they Like One Another?

When spoke about love and relationships, women are found to be so much in love, compared to men. Men take their partners for granted where as women keep building love for the man. When a man is interested in a woman, he is keen to know about her relationship status, he starts showing that her opinion matters to him, he considers her in his decisions, he's curious about her routine, he becomes possessive for her, he would love to protect her in every sense. However, actions speak louder than words, a really interested man invests his time, support and a part of his life for the woman he loves, other wise making excuse isn't a big deal. A man's actions like doing favors, surprising with little presents, showing protectiveness, responsive communication are the gestures that convey if a man loves the woman or not, however, it even depends on the individual, a lot of men are way too inexpressive, even their protectiveness comes out as anger and that's quite tricky for a woman about she has to deal with. It is even possible that a man that does all the above things for the woman can still leave her, for it is easy for men to be attracted to another woman just like that, that's why it has been said that men are more into playful love and women are into serious commitments, however it totally depends on the individual.

It is a lot of time seen how men's feelings change over time, they become less interested in the woman they claimed to love beyond everything else, but it's very common in men that they take women for granted ones they realize that she's his.

Understanding a man is quite tricky as he's often incapable of verbal expression of his emotions. A man's genuine interest is reflected in his actions, his nervousness, but he still makes an effort when he's genuinely interested. A man most of the times have mixed emotions, that's because when he likes a woman he involves her in his future, which makes him confused, nervous and more.

But when a woman falls in love, it is totally different, in the beginning it is very difficult to confess her love, but in case of both being involved in love, it is very easy for her to explain how much she loves her, for women have more verbal capacity than men. She'd align her actions and words very well when she is in love, a woman falls in love deeper and deeper with time, it turns out to be emotional dependency and attachment.

A woman in love will only need a man's love, care and attention, of course there are various wrong assumptions about women that she chooses a man for money where as it is in 99 percent of the cases false, for women too can earn for living but it is companionship, love that women need and not just man's money. Similarly it is mostly misunderstood that men chase women for a physical intimacy, the same can be 99 percent false as well, for there are men that fall in love for companionship, who finds a woman kind to be forever with, no doubt physical connection and intimacy in relationships is a need, but it is not the only need, for it comes after love, trust, companionship, understanding. Both men and women need each other in various different ways, thought each one is financially independent, there are a lot of aspects in which men and women have to be inter – dependent and it cannot be denied.

Nalini couldn't stop herself from recalling how possessive and protective Aadit was, she missed how safe he always wanted her to be, she missed how he was always worried about where and how she is, she just wondered if he doesn't care anymore, for he hasn't contacted her at all. She cried, missing Aadit but maybe it was her ego that didn't want her to text Aadit. But she kept worrying if it was just a misunderstanding between them that kept them separated now. She kept the book aside and kept watching down from the balcony, having the soothing zephyr against her silky hair. After about 28 minutes she moved inside, kept the book on her bed and went in kitchen, to cook some dinner; she cooked a little rice and added to it sautéed veggies and spices. She also ordered some ice – cream, for she wanted to finish reading the last part of the book the same night and then order a new book "LOVE OF MY LIFE" as she loved the cover page of the book.

As the rice was ready to be served, she turned on TV to watch some series, but before that she made a call to Sara, "Hello, how are you? How's Sahaj?", Sara said "Hi Nalini I'm good, Sahaj is recovering, doctor has said he's now out of danger,

I'm very very thankful to the man that has got ready to donate blood in the middle of night, I can never return his favours." "Who was he? So grateful of him" said Nalini, "I don't know Nalini, doctors said that he has asked to not reveal his identity" said Sara, Nalini remembered her dad saying "One should always donate things in such a way that nobody has to know it, he shouldn't boast it" and wondered if it's her dad, but then she denied it assuming there might be so many other men like her dad. Then Nalini said to Sara "okay Sara, take care, will you tomorrow again, when are you coming back?" "I'll come back by Sunday probably, because doctors said Sahaj will be discharged by Thursday, I'll take a leave on Friday, and however there's weekend off, I'll come by Sunday and resume to work on Monday", Sara said. "okay bye" said Nalini and Sara to one another and declined the call. Nalini took the rice on a plate, a glass of water and moved to Lounge to watch series and have dinner, it was 9:23 PM by when Nalini finished her dinner, then she did the dishes by 9:36 PM, by the time she received her ice – cream she was freshening up and getting her skin – care routine for the night done. As she collected ice – cream, she turned on some music, took the book from bedroom and settled on the couch with her favorite beige rug wrapped till her lower abdomen – that was always her comfort position to read, listen to music, watch movies. Listening to the music she continued reading:

How are Men Understood or Misunderstood

A few men are understood, a few of them are misunderstood – in a lot of ways, in a lot of circumstances. No man is same as another, just like each woman is unique from another so are men. As not all women are attention – seekers or gold – diggers, similarly not all men are rapists, playboys. There are men who choose commitment over lust or ludic/playful love, and that happens only when the man finds the woman he'd like to spend his life with, if she's not the woman he genuinely loves, no matter how much the woman loves him, he'd not have second thoughts on leaving her, and that is when women feel like giving up on all men, just because they have met a wrong man at a wrong time. However it might even be possible that he is misunderstood, for usually men are inexpressive and as they bottle up their emotions that can come out as aggression, rage and it is various obvious for the opposite person to feel unloved, uncared, which usually makes women feel a right man will take care rightly; however that is true too – a man would cross oceans or climb mountains for a woman that he genuinely loves, he will love her in her love language, it is not that the two wouldn't have misunderstandings but the man if loves his partner would be ready for inconvenient communications, he'd put efforts to not let her go, but in case she's not the woman he genuinely loves, minor inconveniences too will separate the couple, which will effect the woman's feelings, she'd be hurt, for the entire relationship she will have believed his words and will have actually believed that they'd have a relationship that misunderstandings wouldn't break. Very much well known, misunderstandings break blood relations if not communicated sooner and properly, of course it is not something that would be not affecting other relations.

Generally men are understood to be strong, cold – hearted, where as men will have emotions too, times that they will want to break down too, when even men would need someone to hear, someone to know that they've been working selflessly for family, for everyone they love. Yes, men are of course objective oriented and logical rather than emotional, but all that they are oriented towards achievements is for their family, and not for only themselves. A lot of men might be found selfish but not all of them are.

A man, since he's growing up will take up responsibilities, with a lot of difficulties on way – yet not speaking of any of them to anyone: parents, closest friends. Barely 5 out of 50 men or even less are quite fine with speaking their hearts out for they're raised making them believe that not crying is stronger, men aren't supposed to be soft, where as a man or a woman both have the need of someone that listens, someone that understands.

Of course, the world has become unsafe for women, for every woman has a history or experience of being molested, assaulted, raped. Each rising sun, there's a new case of rape, from a 2 – 3 years baby to 75 – 80 years old lady and of course that is very unsafe for every girl/woman, no government will ever be able to eradicate the increasing rapes, no matter how many laws, for only candle marches happen but the rapists aren't hanged. One of the major disadvantages of laws being only in – favour of women are fake accusations, it might be due to any past revenge or any sort of thing, however neither all men are rapists nor all women do fake accusations.

As a woman's life takes a completely new form as she gets married, it is the same for men too, just that a woman moves to a new place, where as a man almost is misunderstood in his own place, by his own people.

A man is misunderstood for he is not as emotional and communicative as a woman, in every relationship a woman investing more efforts make her feel she's not being loved anymore, and men usually take her for granted when he becomes sure of the woman not leaving him, however as time passes by the woman gets tired of being the only one trying and part ways, which then creates a sense of misunderstanding between the two, where as that is how men and women are, very different yet interdependent. If men where raised like – it's okay to cry even as a boy, they can speak their heart out too – there is always someone to hear you, understand you, you don't have to mask up to be fine all the time, you can feel low too, etc. then men might speak up too, which will become easier for one another to understand each other better. For men being inexpressive, short – tempered, aggressive, they are being understood/misunderstood to be unloving, or they do not care, but a lot of times men's way of expressing their concern is through over – possessiveness which appears toxic, sometimes it's extra protectiveness which becomes restrictive, altogether which ultimately women feel like being controlled and men misunderstanding her to not respecting him for not understanding his concern – combined together both's different point of views it leads to drifts in relationships, which grow high and become a reason for their separation.

As Nalini reads it she remembers how Aadit has always been extremely possessive for her, how he spoke very less but ensured her being safe, he was rude a few times he was a lot concerned about her. She felt, he was inexpressive, he couldn't spend a lot of time with her and that's where she misunderstood him to be unloving and careless about it. She misses him more, she wonders if he's really fine with their separation. She realizes it might just be his inexpressive nature, bottled – up emotions that portrayed him to be rude and un – loving. It was 1:26 AM when she wanted to text Aadit, but she couldn't gather the courage for the same. However she opened his chat window on whatsapp, opened his profile picture and could see a picture of his dad and him together. She missed him, she cried her heart – out, again. With utmost courage, leaving behind what previously happened, wanting to understand him deeper, in point of view of a man, to know him much better, to understand his possessiveness as possessiveness out of love and not controlling, to understand his concern and his love; to even explain him LOVE from a woman's point of view, to explain him how important it is to speak up, how much better it feels to share emotions instead of bottling them up and bringing it out as rage and aggression. However she with all the courage and a deep breathe texted Aadit "Hi", and sent it with a sigh, a sigh of relief or maybe a sigh of confusion or fear.

She kept the phone aside and continued reading the final part of the book

If Men were Raised the Opposite Way Round – A Parallel Universe

Anuv, a 6 year old guy fell from a height of 6 steps and was hurt, he was bleeding and crying out loud, on side was a woman that asked him stop crying like a girl, he's a strong boy and that's where his sister stopped the woman. Anuv's sister let Anuv cry for as long as he wants to, as he cried for 10 mintues, Anuv's sister asked him to stop crying, "I know it's hurting, but let's treat it, you're not a super – hero shown in movies such that falling down won't hurt you, as you cried since 10 minutes, relax now. After she put him some anti – bacterial liquid, she sat beside him and asked him how did he fall? Anuv said "I was walking down the staircase, I tried to skip 2 steps and jump down directly to the third step and I slipped off" Anuv's sister then said, you aren't supposed to do so dear, see now you're hurt out of nowhere. Anuv then felt much better as he spoke out, in case Anuv was only scolded for being mischievous, or if he was only made quiet saying "boys don't cry" probably nobody would know how he fell nor he could cry his heart out for the pain he was feeling.

The book concluded – it isn't just as a six year old, boys being raised this way will have a better verbal expression capability, they can speak their heart out, which wouldn't make them bottle up their feelings and make them angry over the smallest things.

Nalini wanted Aadit to reply a little sooner, she wanted to talk to him a lot of things, she wanted both of them to understand each other better, make their relationship stronger, she wanted them to get back together and make it work better this time, being both of their efforts equal, sometimes 40 – 60 sometimes 60 – 40, a relationship can't always be 50 – 50, when one is a little less, the other has to invest more, however not always the same person can put in more efforts, there has to be mutual understanding and respect. Nalini this time wanted to explain Aadit her love language, she wanted him to know how she wants to be loved; she wanted to love Aadit in his love language, she wanted to know how he wants to be loved, she wanted to know what makes him feel loved, respected. She wanted their love story to be a different kind, one that doesn't drift like it did, she wanted communications and this time she prepared herself to present it all to Aadit and also she wanted and prepared herself to listen every bit of his part, his needs and how he wants their relationship. While waiting for his reply as she turned to the last second page of the book, she dozed off. Her phone received a notification at 4:32 AM and she didn't hear it as she was sleeping, the sleep she fell into after feeling drained crying, feeling of despair – deeper sleep.

Nalini woke up to having book on her tummy, blanket wrapped, and AC on 24 degrees temperature, and a warm lightened lamp. As she woke up, she stretched a few minutes, then rubbed her hands and placed them on her face. She then freshened up and moved to balcony with some lemon tea with added basil leaves. She kept watching the birds – few fly in a pair, few in groups and a few alone, she thought over it, how the birds would fly, how the ones flying alone would feel, she loved the fragrance of morning leaves, the fresh air. As she finished her tea and went to the kitchen, she checked what can she cook for breakfast and lunch, she chopped the required veggies, covered them with a plate and went to take shower. As she moved to bedroom she did the bed, put phone on charging and went to take shower, Aadit's message was unnoticed. As she took shower and got ready, she began cooking some tortilla and a curry, simultaneously some rice. By the time lunch was cooked she made some bread and butter for breakfast. As she was having breakfast, she simultaneously put her sketch book and other stuff into her handbag, she forgot her airpods and almost locked the door, and then rushed back to get the airpods and locked the door and walked downstairs, to walk to towards her office. As she moved down the street she checked her phone then, since morning. She was for a moment shocked to see Aadit has actually replied, she then opened the text that read "Hi Nalini, I hope you're doing good.. I've heard you're working at Enigma Studios Co. in Celestial City, hope everything is fine" she didn't know to reply to the text, she kept reading the text like it was a love letter, she almost cried. Confused about what to reply, Nalini typed "how are you?" and sent it. She wondered why did Aadit text in the mid – night, she worried if he sleeps so late, or wondered if he's waking up that early.

As she reached she again checked her phone if Aadit has replied, she continued to work after she saw he hasn't replied. After half an hour, they had a meeting to attend, as Nalini had to go, she ones checked again if Aadit texted, but she couldn't see his text and felt like she shouldn't have texted it. Then she moved to the conference hall and put her phone on silent, yet she kept waiting for Aadit's text. As the meeting ended she saw Aadit's text and rushed back to her table, grabbed her bag and moved to cafeteria, Saanjh wondered what's up with Nalini, why did rush out that way and didn't even speak to her. Then Saanjh, Abheer, Akshay too moved to cafeteria for lunch, and went to Nalini and asked if something's wrong with her, she said yeah everything's good, just had to attend some text, so rushed here, sorry couldn't talk to you all. Akshay then said "that's not the thing Nalini, we just were worried if something's wrong, anyway, all's well, let's have lunch" Nalini "yeah, okay come let's have lunch" altogether had lunch and moved back to their tables. Throughout, Nalini only recalled Aadit's texts, he had replied "I'm good Nalz, how are you? What's up? I thought you'd never text me, I don't know why you've texted, but I felt a kind of better as I saw your text" Nalini to it had replied,

"I'm fine. Even I didn't know I'd text you, but I did, but why'd you ask it?" waiting for his reply she kept working. As he saw her text he was confused, he just wanted to see her again, he wanted them to get back together, but he was just worried about what Nalini wanted? So he replied, "Why? What do you mean by why? I asked it just like that. By the way where are you staying at?" she replied "I'm staying at Moonlight Meadows Apartment, Ivywood street, Celestial City". He replied, "alone?" she said "no, with Sara". He then texted "I miss you". She didn't know what to reply, she neither was happy nor sad, she just didn't know what to text back. Knowing that she's not knowing what to reply Aadit texted her again "I know things went worse and now you don't know what to reply to my I miss you, but its true about what I said, I'm sorry for what has happened, I don't know what else can I say about it". Nalini then replied, "yeah, I know you cannot tell it how you really feel, I understand that, don't worry. To be honest, I missed you too.." Aadit read the text and was totally speechless, he left the message on read, Nalini felt disguised, she regretted about texting him that, she didn't know if he has ignored her or he got busy. She felt worse about texting it for not receiving a reply even after 3 hours, she felt like deleting it, but he had already read it, she didn't know what to be done, she just kept her phone aside, prepared just one sandwich for dinner and made some mojito herself. It started raining heavily, she felt very bad about texting Aadit, she moved to balcony, she couldn't stop herself from crying, she wished Sara should have been there, she'd have felt better if Sara was there, it was thundering so she moved back to bedroom, and checked her phone again only to know that Aadit hasn't replied. She was irritated, she cried, but washed her face, took the book to finish the last pages:

The last two pages said – "Men and women, both are different in their own ways, men are better in spatial awareness, women perform better in verbal tasks. Women generally are more expressive where as men behave more reserved. Men tend to exhibit higher levels of physical aggression, women engage in relational aggression such as gossip. Women take cautious approaches, where as men do take risks. Women express anxiety and depression and yet seek for help, but men for not being expressive are substance to disorders and antisocial behaviours.

Physiologically men and women are totally different, and no other equality will make both the same and that's one major thing that one needs to understand. No matter how much financially the two become independent, still they're interdependent. Men cannot posses the emotional intelligence that a woman has, women cannot become heavier and want to have any physical fights. Equality is about cerebral equality and never physical and psychological equality. This is something that every individual needs to know.

In any inconvenience women have the freedom to cry, speak out, but when a man does the same it is least bothered. Society has sketched men to be super-power possessing humans, he cannot cry, he cannot be much soft, or whatsoever, a man is considered ideal when he masks up to be a strong, when he fights, when he isn't soft, he is considered feminine if he cares more, if he is soft spoken; where as women can cry about what they're feeling, they can speak out. Doesn't mean all women speak up, there a lot of women that do not speak out, that pretend to be strong, unaffected, but yet if they want to, they can, if not one particular person, still it is acceptable, but to men society itself has assumed to be emotion-less robots. This is why men are built to be very aggressive, disinterested, etc.

Men no matter how real, how good at heart he is, he always considered assumed to be angry, scary, etc. a lot of times men are even considered unsafe, totally acceptable for each and every women has gone through any kind of assault or something, but the same doesn't mean each every single man is a bad man. Very much agreeable that each and every man is at least 10% cold – hearted but not all men are rapists.

Men too go through a lots of things, it is just that it is not being discussed or openly spoken. Women or men, none can live a completely perfect life without one another and that is a matter of fact irrespective of each's financial independence for money cannot fill the spaces that a partner does."

The book then read a poem–

"All around the world as an Iron Man at heart, for if he cries he's asked to thug it up and, be a man.

All around the world to only listen otherwise labelled as an emotionally unavailable man.

All around the world as a statue or a sculpture,

For if he expresses about how he feels he's asked to keep it within and be a

man.

Either way labelled uxorious or a mumma's boy.

Everyone wants to be his first priority, yet he's expected to be a epitome of equality.

He can't be gloomy.

He can't be mushy.

All he's asked to do is to wrap it up and keep it within until he die.

Because he's a man, he can't cry."

She felt so much different about all of this as she read the book, she wondered how a man would lead all his life, trying to satisfy each one in his life without making the other feel left out, unloved. How'd a man do all of it without shedding a single tear, without complaining a single word. Without letting the other know his problems, always up for help, never asking a ear to listen, never selfish when truly loved, never a person that would say a word on what he sacrificed, not a person that'd take off from the responsibility of being a MAN – a son, a husband, a brother, a father, either way misunderstood yet never giving up on any of the one. Truly men are great, maybe not all, but almost all, just like women, men are human too, like not all women are attention-seekers or gold – diggers not all men are rapists too. Yes every women can be a victim of abuse, but not every man is a culprit; for those who are, cannot be a man for real you see, men themselves wouldn't support a creature as such.

Nalini was all tears, she made a call to Abheer, and he was shocked to see Nalini calling him at literally 12:24 AM, as he took call, she cleared her throat to make sure he'd not know she's been crying. "Hello Nalini, what's up? All good? You've called this late..." Abheer said in a worried voice, "Sorry you've been sleeping maybe" Nalini said to which Abheer said "no. no. tell what's up?", Nalini then spoke up, "Abheer actually I wanted to know if you've been with Aadit since our break up, how's he been, what was his behavior, I just want to know everything in detail" Abheer said, "Ya, like I met him after so many years, the only time I had seen him cry was when his dad expired, after that he became a completely changed man, quiet, less social, more focused on family and business, after that he was in grief, he never expressed that to anyone, but his behavioral changes presented it all, no matter how much he masked up, I and another friend of ours understood about it. I exactly don't know when you guys separated but anytime I spoke to him after that, he has been in disbelief about the separation, his behavior, tone of speaking has always made me feel that he cannot accept that you're separated, he is always in a belief that you are living happily without him, he believes his being in your life will impact you, he knows he is extremely protective about you and that makes you feel restricted, he knows he sometimes puts out his feelings in form of anger on you, he knows he's not perfect, but he loves you. He feels after his dad expired, meeting you has brought him back to life in a few ways, as you guys loved each other, you made him miss his dad a little lesser, Nalini he has always expressed you as a very very important person in his life, as you've gone, he has again moved to the grief, despair and aggressive part of his life.. I know you still love him, don't let him go, he is fine only when he's with you.. take care of the man that takes care of everyone.." Nalini couldn't stop crying to know how much Aadit loves her, it is just the typical men behaviour that broke them apart, a little conversation, a better understanding and a few adjustments will keep them together until lives end. "Nothing's wrong Nalini text him or if you don't want to text first I will ask him to do it" said

Abheer, Nalini said “no, no I will let you know about it tomorrow in the office, sorry for disturbing you, thank you so much, good night”, Abheer declined the call saying “okay sure, bubbye goodnight take care, see you tomorrow”. Nalini drank some water, wrapped a pillow in her arms and slipped into sleep.

As Nalini woke to sun glare on her face through the window, she woke, she freshened up, by the time she freshened up she heard the bell ring, she went to collect the milk, but she was stunned to see it wasn’t the milk – man, she couldn’t believe her eyes seeing a bouquet of roses standing before Aadit, tired and drained. She didn’t believe it until Aadit nodded his head to say yes it’s me in real, as he nodded his head with almost tears, he gestured him to get in. He then said “Sorry if you didn’t like me coming here like this, sorry for not informing as well and not replying to your text. I didn’t know what to do when you said you miss me, I needed you back, I felt like I cannot live without you, I know I could have texted you, but I don’t know I just didn’t. So when you texted you miss me, I just couldn’t wait to see you and tell you I love you. I didn’t reply you because I don’t know what I had to say, so I informed at home that I had to go for a day to celestial city and I drove here, I'm sorry if I shouldn't have come". Nalini broke down and hugged Aadit like she has got something she has been wanting since ages, she embossed him tighter with every flowing tear, she cried and broke down, said him "I love you" and wrapped him closer and tighter only to mean she'll never let him go. Aadit shed tears for the first time again after his dad expired, and it was something he couldn't control. After a few minutes, she moved aback and gave him some water, asked him what'd he like to have, he like a gentleman said "Can we spend today, together? Let us begin a new, that will never separate us, please, please take a leave" she said "Yes, we will. I will inform the manager and I'll take shower." He said, "okay". She gave him some fruit juice, took shower and then he freshened up too. As Nalini dressed up in a beautiful maxi, with intricate floral cut-work, and tied her silky hair using a satin scrunchie, accessorizing with a minimal connecting rings neck chain, completing the look with a honeyed pink lipstick, which looked subtle, elegant and perfect on Nalini, Aadit complimented "I feel like I'm seeing you for the first time again and then I've fallen in love with you in the first glance. You look beautiful", "Thank you love" said Nalini. Aadit then asks her if there's any specific place Nalini would like to go or he can drive her as his idea, Nalini chooses the second option. As the two walked downstairs, Aadit and Nalini drove to a peaceful spot quiet towards outskirts of the city. The two loved the weather, as it was drizzling, and a very soft cool zephyr blowing. Aadit had so many plans for the day, as they were driving, they spoke about how these months have been. Alike every time, Aadit was all quiet, Nalini went like "In the first 2 months it was way too difficult, even now it has been, especially since a few days. I always wanted to see you or text you but I always stopped myself from that. I don't know if it was my ego, or whatsoever. I feel like everything's now better." Aadit said "yeah, correct. Same". Nalini realized how Aadit still isn't speaking his heart out, and she said "See Aadit, I know you're a very reserved person, but this time, I want you to know that, I'm not ready for misunderstandings, I want us to speak up things, it's okay to have inconvenient conversations rather than inconvenient distances between us Aadit.. see I know you're strong person, but being strong doesn't mean not speaking heart out or not crying Aadit, bottling up things, not speaking it will only make things worse, I'm not saying only about the relationship, I'm speaking in general. I know you've been through a lot and I want you to speak things out and make your heart lighter, so there's more of calmness and kindness in your heart rather than aggression and rage, which will affect you in the long run and not the other person." Aadit didn't know what he had to say, he typically said, "Nalini you know well this is how I'm, what can I even do about it. And speaking out things to everyone will change nothing." Nalini said, "who asked you to speak things out to everyone? Speak it to me. Or your brother, or your best-friend, speaking to any one person that you feel you can trust will make everything better Aadi, trust me. See no matter what, I'm always always by your side, I'm sorry, I left you previously, but I was just feeling so so done, I too couldn't understand what was I supposed to do, your concern was portrayed through your anger, that made me feel unloved, I couldn't understand your concern behind the anger, you couldn't understand my sensitivity, now through clear communication, no matter how much inconvenient it is, I want both of us to talk out and sort things out before it brings drifts between us, forget that typical 'I'm strong, I don't have to cry, I'm superman' kind of things, you can cry, you can and you should speak up to me about everything and anything, and I love you." "I will try Nalini, it cannot happen in a day or two.. thank you so much for understanding things about me, no I'm not a superman, but men crying isn't good generally, but I thank you for understanding me, showing concern, and thank you for letting me know I have someone that I can speak to when I feel low or disguised, it feels much better to know that you're that person. I'm sorry for losing temper previously, I don't want to lose you", said Aadit. Nalini said "who said that men cannot cry? Get over that misconception Aadi, being a man if you only say that, who else will understand men? How they feel? What they go through? There is no universal rule that men have a super – power to feel-less or not feel anything, or not cry. Even if there is any such rule, how many hell of rules do we humans break? And to break such any rule that is consuming a whole human gender, I don't think it is a crime! Let it go Aadi, just know that you're a human, man doesn't mean to have super-power, a normal human, you men too need to make yourself lighter by talking out, crying or anything other than anger and aggression, crying is normal, aggression or screaming at someone or hitting someone isn't". "Okay Nalini, relax, don't worry; we will align it all."

As Aadit planned, they were driving towards the 'Lillies and Rains' Resort, on the way to the resort he wanted to buy her a present, so did he do the needed, he stopped car behind 'JEWEL OPULENCE' jewelry shop and said her had some work in the office behind the parking and asked her wait for a few minutes. As he walked to the showroom, he checked a few designs and didn't like any of them, he asked for a ring, a very elegant and a different one, he asked for a limited edition ring as he had planned to propose Nalini, however he didn't know if she was ready to accept it or she'd deny it, yet wanted to try his love. He bought a minimal, elegant, diamond ring for Nalini and walked back to the car and they drove to the resort, on the way, Nalini asked Aadit about how he has been, what has he been doing, she told him about her baking workshop, about her new job and about Abheer. Aadit told her about his new start – up, about a his sister's wedding, about his brother's take in business; he even told her he had recently donated blood an accident victim, he roughly could recall the victim's name, and still figured out to say Sahaj; Nalini was happy, shocked and everything to know that it was Aadit who donated blood to Sara's brother, she was proud and a happy person, she fell in love with Aadit a little more to know that her dad and Aadit live by the same principle. She said him it is Sara's brother who he has donated blood to. They spoke of it for a while, and she said how much has Sara been helping her throughout these months of break – up. He apologized to her for leaving her that way, however as they reached resort, he took her to the space he had booked, her favorite kind of place, a water cascade opposite to their table, flowering trees, a beautiful, cozy seats. He ordered her favorite Alfredo Pasta, her favorite mocktail. As she saw him do the little gestures that meant beyond little, she loved how he remembered every detail about her and ordered her favorite food. She totally loved the pasta, it was exactly the same way she wanted, creamiest alfredo pasta, with many veggies – broccoli, bell pepper, and all that she loved. As they had her favorite pasta, Aadit ordered her a desert; so filmy way, so unrealistic way, he kept the ring in the desert plate, with a 'will you marry me, please?' as she sipped some water and opened the desert's cloche, she couldn't believe her eyes and wondered if it is all real? And then as she looked at Aadit almost in tears, he nodded to her, signing that he is for real, the proposal isn't a dream. She said "I love you", he held her hand, took the ring and put it to her hand, she was in happy tears throughout, he fed her the desert that she loved, and then the two spent quality time, after so many months which felt like years passed without one another, she loved the lake view from their room and they had so so much to speak after so long, after 5 hours of time being spent together, they drove back to the city, had some dinner together, and it was 9:12 PM when Aadit wanted to leave for Prithvidur, however after a lot of discussion almost an argument Nalini didn't let Aadit go alone the night for 10 hours drive, she convinced him to stay for the night and go back the next morning. Aadit stayed back the night, they enjoyed the amazing weather in the balcony, cuddling, and nattering all the month's spent without each other, Nalini ordered ice – cream for both of them, the enjoyed the ice – cream, they spoke their hearts out to one another, promised a forever, and cuddled in warm rug, against the cool breeze, "Nalini, I genuinely love you, the most, I'm too expressive by words, but I'd cross oceans for you, I wanna marry you, I will talk about it to my mom immediately as I go back to Prithvidur, Aashitha got married last month, she's married in Celestial City only, but the opposite side of your apartment. As we get married, Nalini you might have to come back to Prithvidur, you will have to take up a lot of responsibilities, but I will always stand by you, I promise" Aadit said, but Nalini keeping her face against his chest, loving his heartbeat, holding his hand like never before, had already dozed off, not knowing how much she heard, he picked her up in his arms and took her to bed, locked the doors, and walked in the room, turned the AC on at 20 degrees and he slept off too, around 3:06 AM Nalini grabbed the rugs as she was feeling cold, he comforted her with the rug and his hug's warmth and turned the AC temperature to 24 degrees – Nalini's comfort temperature, adoring her in sleep, he embossed her and again slept.

Next morning Nalini woke at 6:30 AM, freshened up, prepared breakfast for the two, wrote Aadit a letter and kept it in his shirt's pocket hoping he reads it as he reaches Prithvidur, then she took shower and woke Aadit up, served for themselves breakfast as he freshened up and had the breakfast together, as he was leaving, Nalini couldn't stop herself from crying, and hugging Aadit tighter, "I will not let you go again, ever again, Nalini, I will marry you very soon and then there's no distance, I promise, I don't want you to cry, please, I love you" said Aadit and pecker her forehead, as they smooched, and bid a bye and wished him a safe journey, Nalini hugged him again and he drove towards Prithvidur. After 11 hours and 06 minutes, almost 7:45 PM Aadit called Nalini to inform her he has safely reached and will now talk about her to his mom, she wished him luck, though she was herself tensed about the acceptance or rejection, she prayed to every god she could, she waited for 30 minutes which felt like 30 hours that moment and texted him, he gave no reply, she waited more, then at around 10:23 PM, he called Nalini, "I love youuuu" he said in his happiest tone, Nalini cried happy tears and said "I love you too baby, tell me everything in detail what aunty said", Aadit said "Nalz can I call you tomorrow, I haven't even changed yet, and I'm too tired baby" Nalini said "okay okay no worries, sleep well, bubbye take care, I love you", "I love you too, goodnight take care, lock the doors" said Aadit and the call ended. Nalini texted Aadit as the call ended "Aadi, how do we speak about it at my home?" Aadit replied "Don't worry baby, we will take acre of it, sleep well, I love you". And he changed his dress, and freshened up, to give the dress for laundry he was emptying his pockets, then he found the letter that Nalini had kept, he kept it on his bed to read after he puts them into laundry bag, after he emptied his pockets and put them to the place, he locked the door, turned on the AC and opened the letter "Aadi, I'm sorry for leaving you, you had believed I'd never leave you, but I felt like you took me for granted and bought between us my ego. Anyway, let it go, I now want to tell so much to you baby... I had no expectations that after these months of separation, I'd ever see you or we'd ever get back together, I feel so so so blessed to get us back together, thank you for the ring, the promise and everything Aadi, I'd have not been able to live without you, I love you Aadi. I might have unintentionally hurt you a lot of times, I'm sorry for each of it Aadi, I hope you don't still dislike me for that or something as such. Now that everything has got back to place I will never let you go nor will I ever leave you Aadi. As we've promised to get married, we will start a new life, as soon as our families accept our love, and then, we will live the life we've always dreamt of, I'd do anything for us to get married and I hope you know it.. take care love, text me after you read the letter, here's a piece of poem for you babe – Every sun rise I hope to see with you, every sunset I hope to spend with you;

Today and every tomorrow, all I'd do is love you,

I'd want to spend each day with you,

Your heartbeat is my favorite music,

Your voice is my favorite sound,

Baby to cafune you is my favorite thing,

To embosom you is heaven on earth,

For, to me, you're the man I'd live for,

The man I'd die for"

I love you the most-est Aadit.

Yours,

Love.

Nalini"

Aadit, read it and felt very special, he felt he so much loved by someone, someone is trying to understand him, someone is concerned about him, he felt happy, emotional and all at ones, he took to his phone to text Nalini, he was so tired, but he still managed to type "Hi baby, I'm so over whelmed by the letter, thank you baby, again I cannot express how I feel, but if you were here I could express it with a tight hug to let you know how much I love you and how much this letter meant to, I will treasure this forever just like I will treasure you baby, thank you, goodnight, I love you, I'll call you tomorrow morni" he was still typing and dozed off as he was very much tired, Nalini waited if Aadit has read the letter, she kept waiting for his reply till 1:06 AM and she dozed off without herself realizing. The next morning as Aadit woke and saw he hadn't sent the text, he typed "Good morning my love have a wonderful day, I had read the letter but I dozed off halfway typing a reply to it.. I'm so over whelmed by the letter, thank you baby, again I cannot express how I feel, but if you were here I could express it with a tight hug to let you know how much I love you and how much this letter meant to, I will treasure this forever just like I will treasure you baby, thank you.. call me when you wake up sweety. I love you". And he went to freshen up. Nalini woke up at around 7:12 AM, waking up to a lovely message after so many months made her feel a lot better than the other mornings. She called Aadit as she read the text, he said "Hi babe, however you've a week off, I've booked you flight at 12:00 PM, come to Prithvidur, let's talk to your parents", not being ready and prepared for it Nalini wonders what to do, however Aadit convinces her to catch the flight. Nalini reaches her home by 2:30 PM, freshens up and speaks to her parents about Aadit, however they knew him as a person since many years, the loved the kind of boy Aadit had been, she hadn't expected her parents would accept their love this easily, she hugged them in joy and informed about it to Aadit, he asked both the families to carry forward the required rituals, Aadit informed his sister about it, and she was very much excited to meet Nalini.

3 MONTHS LATER

9TH NOVERMBER

On a dreamy wedding stage stood Aadit and Nalini, Aadit looked more like a cinema hero in his suit, Nalini looked the most stunning bride ever in a mahogany silk saree. Every guest greeting the couple said 'it is a made for each other pair' looking at the two lover birds, in extremely happiest moment of their lives. It was a happy wedding.

One and A Half Year Later

On a Wednesday morning, Nalini had period cramps but had no sign of periods, taking to pregnancy test, she found she was pregnant, as Aadit was at office, she thought she will surprise him as he returns, she then takes shower, goes to her mother- in- law who has been loving her beyond every other person at home, for Nalini never made Aadit's mom feel like she's taking away Aadit from her, Nalini always teamed up rather than considering only herself and Aadit as a family, for she meant her mother – in – law, her brother – in – law, Aadit, his sister, and herself when she said 'FAMILY'. And Aadit's mother loved how Nalini as a person, as wife she is, the smallest arguments and misunderstandings were spoken before they become a huge misconception, Nalini had always with every family member made it sure that hardly in 15 minutes of the argument she speaks up what happened, how she felt it was, how it actually is, she spoke her side of the happening, patiently heard their side and made sure the misunderstanding doesn't bring in distances between the family members, this way she kept the family always made in, no prolonged arguments, no misunderstandings no unsaid conversations, all transparent and a happy family together.

To continue, Nalini walked with the pregnancy result kit to her mother – in – law, she hugged her and showed her the positive result, Nalini called Aadit's sister and informed, she informed her parents. It was a new beginning, a happy moment. Nalini planned a surprise to Aadit and his brother to inform about the pregnancy. She cooked their favorite food, she got them some sweet that her mother – in – law made, as all of them sat on the dining table, Nalini said to her brother – in – law, you shall get married now, the young one will need a 'chachi' soon, both the brothers were confused at first, until Aadit's mom said him, your role is now upgraded from just a husband to dad, Nalini corrected "A son, a brother, and a husband to now even a father" both the brother's felt the happiest than ever before. Aadit hugged Nalini, both together took blessings from Aadit's mom. As they all finished the dinner and had an hour of family time together, chit-chatting, later, Nalini and Aadit moved to their room, Aadit embossed Nalini so so so tight, he was emotional, he was on cloud nine. Nalini wanted a baby boy, Aadit wanted a baby girl. Nalini asked why baby girl, to which Aadit said, "baby boy will be only asked to 'man up', he spoke how men have to live along a lot of things, not everyone will get a partner like you who'd understand men, how they feel, want to listen to their side of stories, etc. I'm lucky babyyy", Nalini said, "even women go through lot of things, Aadi, every individual that takes birth has to go through a lot, nobody can escape the bad nor the good. Aadi, if we have a baby boy na, we will raise him completely different, not like typical man assuming himself as a superman, not expressive, bottling up etc. whatever it is, we shall raise him totally different, we should let him cry instead of saying boys don't cry, we should talk to him daily about how he's feeling and what he's feeling, we shall teach him that it's his responsibility that he makes girls around him feel a sense of safety, we will teach him everything we went through, I will teach him 'JUNE', how men and women are different, how men too can cry and that's totally normal, you teach him how speaking out feels, how will it will help him focus more and achieve more having a calm mind, let us teach him everything that a man can do and isn't wrong, let us teach him psychology, family, love, everything baby". Aadit said "when he has such a beautiful mother, everything is possible", Nalini says "And an amazing father like you will teach him perfect love, perfect man, a man who doesn't always have to bottle up, man is a human not a robot, he can cry too", "Nalz, we teach a hundred things at home, but will the society not put on his shoulders the boulder of 'MAN – UP', OR 'MEN DON'T CRY', or anything as such?" Nalini says "Above all let us teach him, he has a family to look up to not a society to satisfy, for the society is always unsatisfied, no matter what you do, and of course society is all of us, so let us first bring the change in ourselves, slowly will the society change too, or even if it doesn't it's okay; live for and by the family that loves you not the society that judges you". Aadit look at Nalini with eyes filled with tears, almost rolling down and as she wipes his tears and says "I,m always there for you, every moment of your life, I love you" he caress Nalini's stomach, hoping a boy or a girl, both be the human that lives selflessly, loves with no conditions, and always takes care of people around.

Nalini says “don’t worry Aadi, a boy or a girl, the baby that possess your genes will be the best human that stands before all of us, I love you”, “I love you”, says Aadit, looking into each other’s eyes, dreaming of the family further, the baby, and everything, the two, Nalini and Aadit, slip to sleep, holding onto each other, Aadit, carefully hugging Nalini.

Nalini had changed Aadit from a man that was tired of MAN-ING UP, for the good, a lot of bottling up suppresses a person in a lot of untold ways, every physical illness might be cured, but the mental illness – the depression kills slowly, especially when not spoken, when not expressed, every human deserves a ear to hear, every man doesn’t have to be a super – man, men doesn’t have to be robots working, earning but not feeling, men can cry too, when they feel low, they should speak too, and this is not a one day magic, it takes a lot of time, it takes a lot of steps, individual to individual can make magic, to escape tragic like suicides, for mental health is the most precious one, to be taken care with utmost concern, everyone shall speak for themselves, everyone shall speak about how they feel, if not to 3 people at least to one, for every Aadit will find a Nalini, might not be immediately but definitely.

Dear Men

You're the creation with greatest heart.

Raised like you're made to only hear and not be heard.

You're seen as a giver and never the one who needs what you give.

You're raised up like you're made of iron yet expected to be soft, you're not supposed to rust for anything like nothing harms you and hurts you, all that you're wanted for is to give.

Let us bring a change to the society, to the greatest creature let us give a hand to hold, a ear to hear and a heart to understand, to all the men, let us say 'you're no robots, when you don't feel good you can speak your heart out, you can cry too, for a strong man isn't someone who buries everything within but a man that stands against all the odds.

Thank you. The book nowhere meant to ignore women's feelings, for it is very well known, women too go through a lot, the book only meant to focus on men's mental health being ignored but it never meant to ignore women, anywhere throughout, unintentionally if the book's any part has hurt any person, in any way, a sincere apology for causing the pain. Not every woman is a gold – digger, not every man is a rapist; let us consider how men feel, together let us make a change, for MAN – UP isn't a solution for pain, but being there for each other is, 'MEN NEVER CRY' isn't a solution, giving a shoulder to rely on is.

Thank you.

www.ingramcontent.com/pod-product-compliance
Lightning Source LLC
LaVergne TN
LVHW091058150826
845673LV00002B/631

* 9 7 9 8 8 9 5 8 8 9 7 4 9 *